ROMANIA

Romania: Judeţ Borders and Administrative Centers

SLOVAKIA

UKRAINE

MOLDOVA

HUNGARY

YUGOSLAVIA
(SERBIA)

BULGARIA

Black Sea

Satu Mare
MARAMUREŞ
SATU MARE
Baia Mare
BOTOŞANI
Suceava
Botoşani
SUCEAVA
SĂLAJ
BISTRIŢA NĂSĂUD
IAŞI
Oradea
Zalău
Bistriţa
Piatra Neamt
Iaşi
CLUJ
BIHOR
Cluj-Napoca
NEAMŢ
MUREŞ
Bacău
Vaslui
Tîrgu Mureş
HARGHITA
VASLUI
ALBA
Miercurea Ciuc
BACĂU
ARAD
Alba Iulia
Arad
Deva
COVASNA
Sibiu
Sfintu Gheorghe
VRANCEA
GALAŢI
Timişoara
BRAŞOV
Focşani
HUNEDOARA
SIBIU
Braşov
Galaţi
TIMIŞ
Reşiţa
VÎLCEA
ARGEŞ
BUZĂU
Tulcea
GORJ
PRAHOVA
Brăila
CARAŞ-SEVERIN
Tîrgu Jiu
Rîmnicu Vîlcea
Piteşti
Ploieşti
Buzău
BRĂILA
TULCEA
Drobeta-Turnu Severin
Tîrgovişte
IALOMIŢA
DÎMBOVIŢA
BUCUREŞTI
Slobozia
MEHEDINŢI
Slatina
✪ Bucharest
CĂLĂRAŞI
Craiova
TELEORMAN
GIURGIU
Călăraşi
CONSTANŢA
Constanţa
DOLJ
OLT
Giurgiu
Alexandria

- - - - - County (judeţ) boundary
◉ County (judeţ) center
✪ National capital
Bucureşti is a municipality with county status

Romania: Physical Features

SLOVAKIA

UKRAINE

MOLDOVA

HUNGARY

YUGOSLAVIA
(SERBIA)

UKRAINE

BULGARIA

Black Sea

BUKOVINA
Carpathian Mtns.
Someş R.
Bistriţa R.
Bihor Mtns.
TRANSYLVANIA
MOLDAVIA
Siret R.
Mureş R.
Transylvanian Alps
BANAT
Buzău R.
Jiu R.
Olt R.
Argeş R.
Ialomiţa R.
WALACHIA
DOBRUJA
Mouths of the Danube
Danube R.

– – – Regional boundaries

Nations in Transition

ROMANIA

MARK SANBORNE

Facts On File, Inc.

Romania

Copyright © 1996 by Mark Sanborne

Facts On File, Inc.
11 Penn Plaza
New York NY 10001

Library of Congress Cataloging-in-Publication Data

Sanborne, Mark.
   Romania / by Mark Sanborne.
      p. cm. — (Nations in transition series)
   Includes bibliographical references and index.
   ISBN 0-8160-3089-8 (alk. paper)
   1. Romania I. Title.   II. Series: Nations in transition.
DR205.S317   1996
949.8—dc20   95-23517

Facts On File books are available at special discounts when purchased in bulk quantities for businesses, associations, institutions, or sales promotions. Please call our Special Sales Department in New York at 212/967-8800 or 800/322-8755.

You can find Facts On File on the World Wide Web at **http://www.factsonfile.com**

Text design by Cathy Rincon
Cover design by Nora Wertz

Printed in the United States of America

MP FOF 10 9 8 7 6 5 4

This book is printed on acid-free paper.

Contents

Introduction

*R*omania remains an enigma to most Westerners. During the Cold War, Americans tended to think of Eastern Europe as an undifferentiated collection of gray, sullen states suffering under the Soviet yoke. Even with the lifting of the Iron Curtain and the collapse of communism, perceptions have not changed that much. Hungary, Poland, and divided Czechoslovakia are lumped together as modern, if struggling, European states. Bulgaria is thought of as a quiet Slavic backwater. Yugoslavia has become a synonym for bloody tribal chaos. But Romania does not fit into any such neat category, and an air of mystery seems to cling to its history and to its place in the world today. The purpose of this book is to try to explain that enduring mystery.

A recent traveler to Bucharest, Romania's capital, wrote: "Elsewhere in Eastern Europe people debate how much they're part of the 'real' Europe; but Bucharest seems barely to cling to the edge of the continent, threatening to fall off into some other space, some other idea entirely."[1]

Romania is a nation "favored by nature but persecuted by fate," in the words of a 19th-century Russian general.[2] Blessed with natural resources and a hardy, industrious, and proud people, it is also cursed by its geographic location, which has made it a crossroads of intrigue and invasion by a succession of outside powers. From the legions of ancient Rome to the Red Army of the Soviet Union—between which came barbarian hordes, Ottoman Turks, Hungarians, Austrians, Russians, and Germans—Romania has seen a long line of conquerors come and go. But frequently the country's worst enemy has been its own rulers.

Though tucked away in the southeastern corner of Europe, Romania derives its name from ancient Rome; the Romanian language is a Latin tongue, isolated in a sea of Slavic-speaking peoples. Romanians put great stock in their national mythology—which, though exaggerated, is grounded in history—as a people who can trace their roots directly back to the imperial Roman conquest of ancient Dacia. After bringing civilization, the Romans withdrew and left the Dacians to a thousand-year darkness of barbarian onslaughts.

That was the first of many abandonments that have characterized Romanian history—a lament of forever being left alone to face some new enemy. Romanians can perhaps be forgiven for thinking of themselves as a "martyred" nation: They were a Christian land dominated for centuries by the Muslim Turks; their Transylvanian heartland was ruled by Hungarians and the Austrian Habsburg dynasty; they were bullied by an expansionist Russian Empire; they identified with the culture of faraway France but were forced to bow before the power of Germany in two world wars.

Romania has had to perform a delicate diplomatic dance to maintain its national independence since the emergence of the modern Romanian state in the late 19th century. While impressive in its skillfulness, that dance has often infuriated the country's allies, who accused Romania of opportunism in its international affairs. In World War I, Romania began as a secret ally of Germany, switched to neutrality, and finally threw in its lot with the Western Allies. In World War II, after being abandoned by the West, Romania fought on the side of the Nazis before switching back to the Allies at war's end. Then, in what many Romanians viewed as the most treacherous abandonment of all, the Western powers resigned themselves to Romania's domination by the Soviet Union—though some in the West saw that as a fitting punishment for an unreliable ally.

The wheel continued to turn. When Romania began to pull away from the Soviet orbit in the late 1950s and 1960s, at the height of the Cold War, it won back the support of Western nations. As the dictator Nicolae Ceausescu consolidated his grip on power, the West was willing to overlook his dismal domestic record because he was a thorn in the side of the Soviet enemy. The Romanian people as well were initially seduced by Ceausescu's appeals to national pride and independence, until they realized that home-grown tyranny could be just as bad as any imposed from outside.

Through the 1970s and '80s, Ceausescu and his wife, Elena, ruled Romania like dictators from a surreal farce. They exported the country's wealth to pay off foreign debts while the people scrounged for food and huddled without heat or light. Their "pro-birth" policies resulted in hellish orphanages filled with AIDS babies. They tore down picturesque old districts of Bucharest to build huge, spectacularly ugly monuments to their vanity. They established a cult of personality unrivaled anywhere in Eastern Europe. And their secret police, the dreaded Securitate, cast a web of surveillance over the entire society, to the point where many citizens believed everyone was an informer—and perhaps as many as one in every four of them actually was.

The fact that they had to remain silent in their misery made virtually all Romanians feel a mixture of humiliation and impotent rage. There is an old Romanian proverb of Turkish origin: *Saruta mina pe care nu o poti musca*, or "Kiss the hand you cannot bite." Over the centuries it could be applied to Romania's relations with its various Ottoman, Hungarian, German, and Russian overlords. Above all, however, it is an apt metaphor for Romanians' cowed collaboration with their own misrule at the hands of Ceausescu. The fact that such continuity is understandable in the light of Romania's history does not make it any less tragic.

The depth of the repression and the pent-up rage, combined with the huge gap between Ceausescu's rhetoric and the country's dire reality, ensured that the regime's end would be an explosive one. Unlike Eastern Europe's other Communist governments, which fell with barely a whimper, Romania's went out with a definite bang in December 1989. The paradox is that the dramatic "revolution" against Ceausescu was both the bloodiest and yet in some ways the least politically decisive of the East's upheavals.

More than 1,000 people were killed, including the dictator and his wife. But the faces in the National Salvation Front that took over the reins of power looked suspiciously familiar to many Romanians. That raised questions and conspiracy theories that continue to echo in Romania today. Is the revolution only "half-finished"? Was a genuine popular uprising "hijacked" by a neocommunist cabal of Ceausescu holdovers to preserve their powers and prevent real reform and genuine democracy?

More generally, what has changed in Romania since 1989 and what has not? At least on the surface, Romania today enjoys more political and social freedom than it ever has before, but it has been slower to move toward a genuine free market economy than any other East European state. So the short answer is: A lot has changed, and a lot has not. The long answer is to be found in the rest of this book. The first part covers the country's history from ancient times through the end of communism, knowledge of which is vital to any understanding of the Romanian "mystery." The second part deals with Romania's rocky transition to democracy and with life in the country today. The final chapter makes a brief attempt to assess Romania's future prospects.

It is a tale of blood and pride, heroes and tyrants, hope and despair. And it is one that—judging by Romania's long and colorful history—will not be ending any time soon.

NOTES

1. Eva Hoffman, *Exit into History: A Journey Through the New Eastern Europe*, p. 290.
2. Edward Behr, *Kiss the Hand You Cannot Bite*, p. 34.

PART I

HISTORY OLD & NEW

1

The Lay of the Land

It has been said that geography determines history, and this is especially so in the case of Romania. Its location in southeastern Europe, in the northeast corner of the Balkan Peninsula, puts it astride one of the great migration and invasion routes from East to West. It lies halfway between Europe's westernmost point, the Atlantic coast of Portugal, and its easternmost, the Ural Mountains of Russia.

Although it has been both larger and smaller through the centuries because of its tumultuous history, the modern Romanian state has an area of 91,699 square miles (237,500 square kilometers), making it almost the size of the state of Oregon or the United Kingdom. Its greatest distances are about 450 miles (720 km) from east to west and 320 miles (510 km) from north to south. It is bordered in the northwest by Hungary, in the southwest by Serbia (part of the former Yugoslavia), in the south and southeast by Bulgaria and the Black Sea, and in the east and north by the former Soviet republics of Moldova and Ukraine.

The landscape consists of about one-third mountains, one-third uplands (hills and plateaus), and one-third plains. There is an extensive system of rivers, most of which feed into the mighty Danube that forms Romania's southern border. The Danube is the country's economic lifeline, irrigating land for farming and providing a vital commercial transport link to the rest of Europe. As the fabled waterway enters the southwestern corner of Romania, it rushes through a series of narrow gorges known as "gates," the most famous of which is the Iron Gate. Today the river has been partially tamed with a series of locks and dams, but traces still remain of the stone bridge the Romans built during their invasion of Dacia in A.D. 106.

If the Danube is Romania's lifeline, the Carpathian Mountains are its soul. This range forms a great semicircle, running from the north through the center of the country and ending in the southwest. It is divided into the Eastern, or Moldavian, Carpathians and the Southern Carpathians, more commonly known as the Transylvanian Alps. The somewhat lower Bihor Massif is located in the northwest. The country's highest point, Mt. Moldoveanu in the south, is 8,343 feet (2,544 meters) above sea level.

The Carpathians are crisscrossed by a series of high river valleys and summit passes that make them easier to traverse than most European mountain ranges. Although well-settled, many of the lower slopes are still covered with dense forests, which are home to wild boar, chamois (a goat-like antelope), bears, and wolves.

Thanks to Hollywood and Gothic literature, this region of Romania is known in the West mostly for its legends of vampires and werewolves. While these mountains are indeed a source of local myth and folklore, their real importance for Romanians has been their historic role as a natural refuge during times of danger and oppression. The mountains were a symbol of national resistance, where peasants could escape the harsh rule of the feudal lords of the lowlands, and where Romanians could retreat in the face of foreign invasion.

The Carpathians also serve a more basic function: regulating the country's weather patterns and climate. The mountain barrier restricts Atlantic air masses to the west-central area of the country, resulting in higher rainfall and milder winters there. At the same time, they block the air masses moving in from the Eurasian plain, so that the southern and eastern portions of the country get less rainfall, colder winters, and hotter summers. Annual precipitation varies from more than 50 inches in the mountains to less than 20 inches in the lowlands. Bucharest, the capital, is situated inland on the southern plain and averages temperatures of about 27 degrees Fahrenheit (–3 degrees Celsius) in January and 73 degrees F (23 degrees C) in July.

To understand Romania's history, one must first become acquainted with the country's three major regions (Moldavia, Walachia, and Transylvania) and three other smaller regions (Banat, Bukovina, and Dobruja). They no longer serve any real governmental function, as the highly centralized modern state is officially divided into 42 separate *judete*, or districts. But these six diverse regions, each with its own distinct geography and history, remain for Romanians the most meaningful divisions of their country.

Moldavia, located in the northeast, stretches from the Eastern Carpathians to the Prut River, which forms the border with what used to be the Soviet Union. (The Prut is known in Romanian as the *riu blastemat*, the "accursed river," because over the centuries so many invaders from the Eurasian steppes crossed it on their way west, pausing only to slaughter the local peasants and lay waste to the countryside.) Ranging from high peaks in the west to a level plain in the east, Moldavia is the most heavily forested part of Romania.

Farther east, between the Prut and Dniester rivers, lies the region formerly known as Bessarabia, after a 14th-century Moldavian prince, Bessarab. Long contested for by the Turks, the Russians, and the Romanians, this territory today is the formerly Soviet and now independent republic of Moldova, the majority of whose population are ethnic Romanians. It was briefly united with Greater Romania during the period between World Wars I and II.

Walachia runs south from the Transylvanian Alps to the Danube River. It is divided by the Olt River into two regions. The larger eastern section is known as Muntenia; Bucharest is located there. The smaller western section is known as Oltenia. Blessed with rich soil and well-watered by the Danube's floodplain, Walachia contains the country's best farmland.

On the other side of the great curve of the Carpathians lies the "land beyond the forest"—Transylvania. It stretches from the center of the country to the northwest and consists mostly of rolling plains and low hills. Although its soil is poorer than Walachia's, it is still an important agricultural region and also contains large deposits of natural gas and salt.

Transylvania is home to a sizable minority of ethnic Hungarians, and control of the disputed region has shifted back and forth over the centuries between Hungary and Romania.

Banat, which means "frontier province," is a fertile plain located in the southwest corner of Romania. It is bounded by the Transylvanian Alps in the east, the Danube in the south, the Tisza River in the west, and the Mures River in the north. In the opposite corner of the country, the northeast, is Bukovina, a mountainous, forested region between the Carpathians and Moldavia, to which it was attached politically in ancient times. Romanians, Jews, Ukrainians, Poles, and Germans lived together there in a cosmopolitan culture; one writer described the Bukovina of his youth as "a country inhabited by people and books."[1] It came under the control of Austria for several centuries, and its northern portion was seized by the Soviet Union earlier in this century.

Finally there is Dobruja, a marshy area in Romania's southeast corner along the Black Sea coast. Bulgaria has controlled this region at times in the past. Its northern part consists of the vast Danube River delta, which provides much of the country's fish production. It also contains a wildlife preserve that offers refuge to many rare plant and animal species, particularly waterfowl. Today this unspoiled part of Romania serves as a magnet for migrating birds. But in ancient times, the country as a whole attracted less welcome migrations of a different sort, as we shall see in the next chapter.

Romania's geography has shaped Romanians' views of themselves, as many of the country's intellectuals and artists have noted. "A national history consisting of a series of catastrophes, a geographic position at the crossroads of East and West, directly in the path—and at the mercy—of interests more powerful than one's own: all this probably teaches caution," writer Norman Manea observed. "What can you do? You have to survive."[2]

But if the land has been a cause for misfortune, it is also a source of deep emotion, especially to those who have left it behind when fleeing into exile. The poet Andrei Codrescu wrote, "There is an untranslatable Romanian word that expresses with great precision the kind of unbearable longing and nostalgia that grips one's heart when thinking of home. That word is *dor*. I have felt it many times."[3]

When Codrescu returned to his beloved homeland after the 1989 revolution, he made a pilgrimage to his birthplace in Transylvania. He wrote:

We passed small villages dominated by spires of wooden churches. Now and then we saw roadside shrines, big stone crosses with little huts to pray in. They marked places where travelers died, where battles were fought, where miracles occurred. The country we were driving through had seen thousands of years of wars, conquests, refugees, invasions, migrations. The simple faith embodied in the roadside shrines kept the people going through all of it.[4]

NOTES

1. Norman Manea, *On Clowns: The Dictator and the Artist*, p. 23.
2. Ibid, p. 17.
3. Andrei Codrescu, *The Hole in the Flag*, p. 177.
4. Ibid, pp. 150–151.

2

From Ancient Times to the Early Modern State

*T*o begin at the beginning: There is archaeological evidence of human habitation of the territory of present-day Romania as far back as 100,000 years ago, when Neanderthal people huddled in caves across Europe amid the advancing and retreating glaciers of the Ice Age. In late Neolithic (New Stone Age) times, the local population became intermixed with invading

Indo-European nomads from the east, eventually giving rise to the tribes known by the early Greeks as Thracians.

Beginning in the seventh century B.C., Greek colonists founded settlements along the Black Sea coast of Dobruja near the mouth of the Danube, at Tomi (present-day Constanta) and Callatis (today's Mangalia). The Greeks traded with and influenced the culture of the Getae, a relatively advanced Thracian tribe living north of the Danube. Although a sedentary people, living in villages and raising crops, the Getae were not averse to fighting. Ovid, the famous Roman poet who was exiled to Tomi (he died there in 16 A.D.), wrote that the Getae farmers had to wield a sword in one hand while steering their plows with the other in order to defend themselves from raids by fierce Scythian horsemen from the Eurasian plains.

The Roman Conquest

Eventually, the Getae organized themselves into a kingdom, and found themselves in conflict with the growing power of Rome, which had succeeded ancient Greece as the major civilization of the Mediterranean basin. The Romans referred to the Getae lands as Dacia, and coveted them for their gold and silver mines and agricultural plenty.

Two centuries of back-and-forth skirmishes and treaties followed the Dacians' bold invasion of Roman territory in the western Balkans in 112 B.C. Finally, Emperor Trajan decided that Rome had had enough, and in A.D. 101 he launched the first of his campaigns to subdue Dacia, building bridges across the Danube and conquering its southern portions—Banat and Walachia. After the restless Dacians rebelled under their great king, Decebalus, Trajan finished the job in a hard-fought war in A.D. 105–106, capturing the heart of the Dacian kingdom in Transylvania.

The importance of the victory to the Roman Empire was commemorated by the erection of the famed Trajan's Column in Rome, an imposing monument that still stands today, decorated with raised bas-reliefs showing detailed scenes of the conquest. (A similar, though smaller column was raised at Adamclisi in Dobruja.)

The Romans named their newest province Dacia Felix—Happy Dacia— and for the next century and a half it played an important role in their

A memorial built in honor of the ancient Dacian king Decebalus, who fought the Romans in A.D. 105–106. (Romanian Tourist Board)

empire, supplying it with grain, gold, silver, and other minerals. The Romans imported colonists from all across the empire, some of whom undoubtedly intermarried with the Dacians. The newcomers built roads and cities, the ruins of which can still be seen today. But the most permanent legacy Rome left was her language.

The Vulgar, or common, Latin of the garrisoned troops and colonists first became the language of administration and commerce and gradually became widely spoken by the entire populace. By the time Rome withdrew from Dacia, its people had a common language, one of the few unifying characteristics that would provide the Daco-Romanians with a national identity through the millennium of turmoil and upheaval that was to come.

The importance of this legacy cannot be overemphasized. The name Romania obviously derives from Rome, and modern Romanians are fiercely proud of their heritage from classic civilization, believing it sets them apart from—and above—their benighted neighbors. Although it has absorbed many Slavic words, modern Romanian is a Romance language, like Italian or French, and thanks to the persistence of the mother tongue of the Roman legionnaires, Romania today remains a "Latin island" in a sea of Slavic and Magyar (Hungarian) languages.

Not all the people of the region were "happy" with Rome's domination, and the province continued to be harassed by "free Dacians" from the north and east who allied themselves with other warlike tribes. When the great migrations of barbarian hordes from the Eurasian plains began in the mid-third century, Rome realized its defensive borders were overextended. In A.D. 271, Emperor Aurelian ordered Roman soldiers and colonists to withdraw south of the Danube.

The Dark Ages: Invasions from the East

Some of the colonists probably stayed behind, although there is no firm record of this. In fact, there is little documented history at all of what occurred in Romania in the dark ages that followed, leaving much room for speculation by historians. What is known is that a seemingly unending series of invasions occurred, first by Germanic tribes: Visigoths, Huns, Ostrogoths, Gepids, Lombards, and Avars.

From the third to the sixth centuries, the sequence was the same. Fierce bands of warriors would sweep across the countryside, pausing on their way to richer lands to the west and south, imposing a brutal but temporary occupation. Before they could become firmly established or leave anything of importance behind, another horde would descend from the east, pushing out the previous occupants.

What became of the original Daco-Romanian population during this dismal period is an open question, although it is thought that many of them may have hidden themselves in the Carpathian Mountains, a natural sanctuary from rampaging horsemen. Meanwhile, in the more accessible regions, the Roman towns were abandoned, the roads built by Roman engineers crumbled from disuse, and peasant life in the countryside degenerated into a grim cycle of violence and hunger.

Beginning in the sixth century, and continuing over the next 300 years, the former Dacian lands were flooded with fresh waves of immigration, this time by Slavic tribes. The Slavs, however, came not as conquerors but mostly as land-seeking peasants who settled in villages and intermarried with the Daco-Romanians. Aside from their contributions to the Romanian language, the Slavs also brought another key influence: religion. Farther south, the Slavs founded the Bulgar Empire, which in 676 absorbed much of the southern reaches of ancient Dacia. After the Bulgars converted to Christianity in 864, the Romanians followed suit, adopting the Slavonic-language rite of what later became the Orthodox Church, a rite they maintained until the 17th century, when Romanian became the language of the Orthodox liturgy.

Magyar Rule in Transylvania

The last of the major invasions from the east that was to have a lasting effect on Romanian history occurred in 896, when the Magyars—a Mongolian-Finnish tribe—arrived and settled in the Pannonian Plain north of the Carpathians. They founded the kingdom of Hungary. A century later King Stephen I integrated Transylvania, the heartland of ancient Dacia, into his domain.

From that moment on, the history of the region became entangled with issues of ethnicity, religion, and political power that continue to have repercussions today. Hungarian nationalists, seeking to establish their claim to Transylvania, maintained that when the Magyars arrived there the land was essentially empty—that the Dacians of antiquity had fled or been driven out by the barbarian invasions. This appears to be an untenable claim, however. Hungarian chronicles refer to Magyar struggles with the original inhabitants of the area, the "Vlachs"—a Slavic word derived from the Germanic denoting the region's Romanized population, and the linguistic root of "Walachia."

The ethnic differences were compounded in 1054 when the Eastern Orthodox Church of Byzantium, the intact eastern portion of the old Roman Empire, centered in present-day Turkey and Greece, split from the western Roman Catholic Church. The Magyars were converted to Roman Catholicism and remained faithful to it after the schism, while most of the Romanian and Slavic peoples continued to follow the Eastern Orthodox rite.

The Magyars were not numerous enough to consolidate Hungarian control over Transylvania, so King Stephen and his successors invited foreign colonists to help them settle the territory. These consisted mostly of Szeklers, an offshoot of the Magyars, and Germans, who were known as Saxons. Remnants of both of these populations survive in Transylvania today and maintain their distinctive cultures.

The Hungarians also recruited noblemen from the orders of Western knighthood that had fought in the Christian Crusades against Muslim control of the Holy Lands in Palestine. A feudal order was established as the Hungarians granted land, commercial privileges, and political autonomy to the foreign settlers at the expense of the Vlachs, the native Romanian inhabitants. Only Roman Catholics were allowed to be nobles, and while some Romanian noblemen converted to Catholicism to maintain their stature, most Romanians were peasants who remained loyal to the Orthodox faith. They became, in essence, fourth-class citizens in their own land, their status even lower than that of the Catholic serfs of Magyar and Germanic descent.

This process was accelerated after the brief but calamitous Mongol invasion of 1241–42, which saw the horde led by the offspring of Genghis Khan sweep through Eastern Europe, defeat all the armies arrayed against it, and lay waste to the countryside, slaughtering much of the population. Transylvania was particularly hard-hit, and after the Mongols withdrew suddenly, the Hungarian king invited more foreigners to settle the devastated region and ordered them to build fortresses. The long-term result was that Transylvania achieved autonomy from the Hungarian kingdom as the local nobles gained greater powers, seized more peasant land and increased feudal obligations.

After a bloody uprising by both Romanian and Magyar peasants in 1437, Transylvania's noblemen formed the Union of Three Nations, which reduced all peasants to serfdom and recognized the nationality and privileges of only three groups: Magyars, Szeklers, and Saxons. Romanians and all others were only "tolerated," and even Orthodox priests were reduced to servitude.

Yet another peasant rebellion erupted in 1514. Numerous but disorganized, the rebels were again ruthlessly suppressed by the forces of the united nobles. The rebel leader was executed in a famously grisly fashion in the western Transylvanian town of Timisoara: He was seated on a "throne" of red-hot iron and a similarly scorching "crown" was placed on his head. His body was then torn to pieces and put on display in various towns. So many of his followers—both Romanian and Magyar—were killed that for years afterward the Hungarians could not find enough peasants to recruit into their army, thus contributing to their subsequent defeat at the hands of the invading Ottoman Turks.

The subsequent Turkish conquest brought no relief, as the Ottomans allowed the Hungarian nobles to keep their feudal system intact. In Hungary itself, the peasants' freedom of movement was restored a few decades later, but hereditary serfdom continued in Transylvania until the late 18th century, while a similar situation existed in Moldavia and Walachia.

The Rise of Moldavia and Walachia

Ironically, the Magyar and Catholic domination of Transylvania served as the impetus for the founding of the voivodates (principalities) of Moldavia and Walachia in the 14th century, laying the foundation of the modern Romanian state. Ambitious Vlach noblemen, kept from power by their Romanian nationality and Orthodox faith, crossed the Carpathians into the forested regions of the east and the Danube basin to the south, where the political vacuum created by the Roman withdrawal had never really been filled. These émigré noblemen filled the gap by setting up their own power bases where they could lord it over the local peasants. They were joined by peasants fleeing the intolerable conditions of serfdom in Transylvania, although they found conditions in these new lands scarcely more comfortable.

Under their new princes, or voivodes, Moldavia declared its independence from Hungary in 1360, and Walachia followed suit in 1380. The Magyars tolerated these primitive new states as barriers against incursions from the east and south, and the Vlach nobles were obliged to pay homage to the Hungarian sovereign. But for the most part the princes were left to rule as they saw fit.

Despite the relative peace that reigned during this initial period, life in Moldavia and Walachia was far from enviable. At a time when England had a functioning parliament and Dante was composing his *Divine Comedy* in Italy, the Romanian lands were in an extremely backward state. There were no significant towns. Peasants lived in villages of mud-wattle huts and dressed in the same rustic clothes that had been illustrated on Trajan's Column a thousand years before. There was a complete lack of education, and even religion was poorly organized. Italian merchants from Venice and Genoa founded commercial settlements along the Black Sea coast, but trading was left in the hands of Greeks, Armenians, Jews, Poles, and Germans, while the native Romanians restricted their economic pursuits to simple agriculture.

The Rise of the Ottoman Turks

In the early 14th century, the Ottoman Turks began their rise to power in Anatolia (today's Turkey). Over the next 100 years, they expanded and steadily chipped away at the already reduced power of Byzantium, the former Eastern Roman Empire, until finally only its capital, Constantinople (present-day Istanbul), remained as the sole Christian outpost in a Muslim sea.

The Turks crossed the Bosporus Strait into southeastern Europe in 1352, taking control of the region known as Thrace, which included Greek, Macedonian, and Bulgarian lands. In 1389, the Turks won a historic battle against the Serbs at Kosovo, and four years later they crossed the Danube for the first time and entered Walachia.

According to some accounts, one of Walachia's few capable and strong princes, Mircea the Old (1386–1418), had sent troops to fight alongside the Serbs at Kosovo. Afterward, the Turkish sultan had Mircea seized and held until he promised to pay tribute to the Sublime Porte (gate), which was the name given to the Ottoman government. Unhappy as a vassal, Mircea fled to Transylvania and enlisted the support of Hungary's King Sigismund for a Christian crusade against the "infidel" Turks. The campaign failed, and Sigismund's forces were soundly defeated at Nicopolis, in present-day Bulgaria, in 1396.

Mircea and his mostly peasant soldiers survived the rout and escaped back across the Danube. There followed a brief respite. The Turks returned to the Balkans in 1417 and forced an overmatched Mircea to pay tribute and surrender territory to the Porte. In exchange, Walachia was allowed to remain a principality and keep its Orthodox faith. Mircea, described by one German historian as "the bravest and ablest of the Christian princes," died the following year.[1]

Over the next 25 years in Walachia and Moldavia there was a succession of 11 princes, as both Hungary and Poland schemed to put their own men in power. The Ottomans' capture of Constantinople in 1453 gave the Turks control of the Black Sea, halting Venetian and Genoese trade in the region and increasing the isolation of Walachia and Moldavia. But Hungarian forces led by Janos Hunyadi then proceeded to rout the Turkish army outside Belgrade (in modern-day Yugoslavia) in 1456. The victory delayed the Ottoman march on Central Europe for decades, although Hunyadi died of plague shortly after the battle.

Before his death, Hunyadi installed Vlad Tepes as prince of Walachia. He became the infamous Vlad the Impaler. Vlad, who ruled from 1456 to 1462, won his nickname by his gruesome habit of impaling his wriggling enemies—particularly Turks—on high pointed stakes, leaving them there to die slowly.

Vlad was also a capable military commander who won a number of victories against the Turks during his relatively brief reign. However, in creating a centralized, powerful army, he suppressed and alienated many of the boyars, or nobles, who ultimately turned against him. The Turks drove Vlad into exile in Hungary and replaced him with his brother, Radu the Handsome, who served as a docile instrument of the Porte. When Vlad tried to stage a comeback in 1476, the Turks gained their revenge by capturing him, decapitating him and, fittingly, displaying his head on a stake. Walachia ceased opposing Ottoman inroads, and the main theater of resistance shifted to Moldavia.

The Real Dracula?

Although a number of bloodthirsty Romanian tyrants have earned the sobriquet "Dracul" (Devil) over the centuries, it is Prince Vlad Tepes—better known as Vlad the Impaler—who seems to have provided the main historical prototype for Bram Stoker's classic 1897 vampire tale, *Dracula*. (In the novel, the Transylvanian count claims to be a Szekler boyar descended from Attila the Hun.) "Every known superstition in the world is gathered in the horseshoe of the Carpathians, as if it were the center of some imaginative whirlpool," Stoker wrote.[2] He apparently mixed the tales of Vlad's grisly tortures with a real-life 17th-century "vampire," Elizabeth Bathory, a Hungarian countess famous for having murdered 600 young girls and bathed in their blood to retain her youthfulness.

Modern Romanians have an ambivalent attitude toward Vlad Tepes. On the one hand, he is celebrated as a national hero for his blows against the Turks, and it is claimed that his reputation for viciousness is mostly black propaganda concocted by his Hungarian contemporaries to distract attention from their own failure to resist the Turkish onslaught. On the other hand, recognizing the tourist value of the "vampire" mystique, Romanian authorities tout Bran Castle—located southwest of Brasov in Transylvania—as "Dracula's Castle," the historic redoubt of Vlad the Impaler, although in fact he apparently spent a total of only two weeks there while on the run from his many enemies. The castle is currently in danger of collapse due to cracks in its foundation.

Crumbling, mysterious Bran Castle in Transylvania. Touted as "Dracula's castle," it served as a brief resting stop for Vlad Tepes (the Impaler). (AP/Wide World Photos)

Stephen the Great and Michael the Brave

The defeat of Vlad Tepes in Walachia set the stage for the rise of a Romanian national hero, Prince Stephen the Great, who ruled Moldavia from 1457 to 1504. His ceaseless efforts to defend his homeland against foreign inroads, although ultimately unsuccessful, have left him with an esteemed place in Romanian history and folklore, similar to that of the celebrated heroine of medieval France, Joan of Arc.

At this point, Moldavia technically owed allegiance to the king of Hungary, while its geographic location placed it within the sphere of influence of the Polish kingdom. In addition, it faced attack from the barbarian Tartars to the east, all the while being confronted by the greatest threat of all: the continuing, centuries-long march into Central Europe by the Ottoman Turks. Stephen owed his success to his skills as a guerrilla warrior who chose his battles carefully and played his stronger enemies against each other.

Stephen's overriding interest was to use Moldavia as an independent base to defend Christianity against the Muslim advance. To that end, he attempted to ease feudal divisions within Moldavia by centralizing the state under his control. He is also remembered as a patron of the arts who sponsored a renaissance of Moldavian religious culture, including the building of a number of strikingly beautiful churches and monasteries—filled with a unique collection of Orthodox frescoes, tapestries, and parchment manuscripts—which survive to this day.

Stephen's reputation as a champion of the common people enabled him to raise a 55,000-man peasant army, which, combined with his astute generalship, gave him a potent weapon to wield against his foes. One chronicler described Stephen thus: "Master of the craft of war, he went wherever he was needed so that seeing him his men would not disperse and for that reason there was seldom a war that he did not win. And when others defeated him, he did not lose hope, for, when vanquished, he would rise above his vanquishers."[3]

In the 1480s, first Hungary then Poland signed peace treaties with the Ottoman sultan (king), and the Turks captured the strategic Black Sea fortress of Chilia, the "key to the door to all Moldavia as well as Hungary and the whole Danubian region."[4] Abandoned by his erstwhile allies, Stephen ceased his anti-Turkish crusade, and on his deathbed allegedly advised his son, Bogdan the One-Eyed, to come to terms with the infidels if they offered an honorable peace. Wasting no time, soon after Stephen's

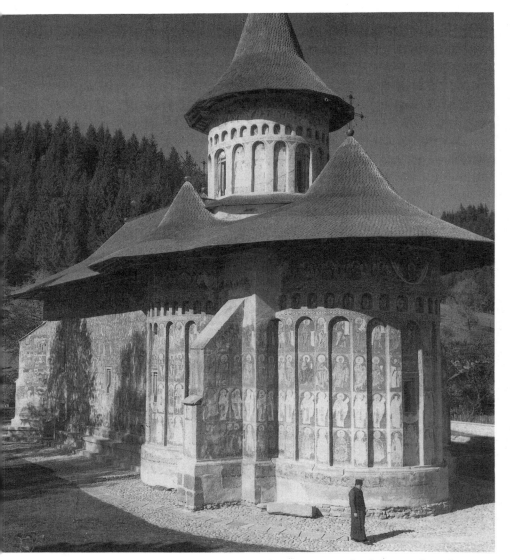

The famous monastery at Voronet in Bukovina. It was built by Stephen the Great in 1488; the painted frescoes were added later. (Romanian Tourist Board)

death in 1504 Bogdan signed a treaty of vassalage with the Sublime Porte, although periodic acts of resistance persisted in the decades that followed.

Stephen the Great's successes have inspired generations of Romanians down to the present day. His eventual failure, however, helped feed a belief that has continued to haunt the national consciousness: that Romania's interests have been consistently betrayed over the centuries by the cynical manipulations of outside powers.

Hungary, meanwhile, which had been weakened internally by peasant revolts and feudal tensions, proved an irresistible target to the ascendant Turks. They captured Belgrade in 1521, won a pivotal victory over a Hungarian army at Mohacs in 1526, and seized Buda (later Budapest) in 1541. As a result of these conquests, Transylvania became an autonomous principality under Ottoman vassalage, while both Walachia and Moldavia lost their few remaining vestiges of independence.

Turks were not permitted to own land or build mosques to spread the Muslim faith in the two principalities, due to their status as vassal states rather than *pashaliks* (provinces of the Ottoman Empire). But the Ottomans, in league with their local rulers, did allow Turkish and Greek merchants and usurers (moneylenders) to systematically exploit the region's wealth, which had the effect of smothering the small Romanian middle class and further impoverishing the peasantry.

This was the situation that existed at the time of the brief reign of Michael the Brave (1593–1601). He began his rise to power in the traditional manner, by paying a huge bribe to the Porte to win appointment as prince of Walachia. But unlike the mostly servile rulers who preceded him, Michael's goal was total independence from the Ottoman Empire.

Shortly after being enthroned, he signaled the start of his revolt by rounding up a group of Turkish moneylenders, locking them in a building, and burning them alive. He then proceeded to lead his army in a successful campaign against Turkish military forces in Walachia. Searching for allies, in 1598 he pledged loyalty to Holy Roman Emperor Rudolf II, the ruler of Austria's Habsburg Empire. The following year he marched on Transylvania, routing the Hungarians there, and in 1600 he went on to conquer Moldavia. Michael proclaimed himself "Prince of Walachia, Transylvania and Moldavia," and for the first time the lands that would ultimately comprise the modern state of Romania were united under one ruler.

Although Michael's moment of triumph did not last long, the example he set served as an inspiration for Romanian nationalists in the centuries that followed. His tale, however, was not necessarily the purely idealistic and heroic epic related by later Romanian chroniclers. In common with the princes and politics of his era, Michael's success was built as much on treachery and betrayal as it was on bravery and military skill.

In the end, it was Michael's unexpected success that led to his undoing. Alarmed by his growing power, Emperor Rudolf prompted Transylvania's nobles to launch their own revolt against Michael, while at the same time Polish forces, allied with the Turks, intervened in Moldavia. Michael was assassinated in 1601 on the orders of Georgio Basta, the Habsburg emperor's general. For a prince with such a short-lived career, his legacy was a long-lasting one.

Transylvania under Habsburg Rule

For 150 years, from 1540 to around 1690, Transylvania enjoyed an era of autonomy as the mostly Hungarian nobles ruled the country with little interference from their nominal Ottoman overlords. Meanwhile, the 16th-century Reformation—the anti-Catholic religious movement that led to the establishment of Protestant churches and sects throughout Europe—found particularly fertile ground in Transylvania.

In 1571 the Transylvanian Diet (parliament) passed a law granting equality and freedom of worship to the country's four "received," or officially recognized, religions: Roman Catholic, Calvinist, Lutheran, and Unitarian (a liberal Protestant sect that rejected many standard Christian doctrines). Although the law was progressive for its time in Europe, it had one glaring inconsistency: It failed to recognize the Orthodox faith of the Romanians, who remained the largest religious subgroup in Transylvania.

In 1683, the Ottoman advance into Europe crashed futilely against the gates of the Austrian capital of Vienna, after a long siege where united Christian forces defeated and drove off a huge Turkish army. As the Turks' power was gradually rolled back in the decades that followed, the Transylvanian Diet in 1688 renounced the Ottoman overlords and ac-cepted the rule of Austria's Habsburg Empire. Habsburg control over

Transylvania, formalized by the Treaty of Karlowitz in 1699, was to last the next two centuries.

Religious issues and conflicts continued to dominate during this period. The most important development, in terms of Romanian history, was the creation of the Uniate Church in 1699. The Uniate Church (not to be confused with the Unitarian faith) retained most of the rituals and liturgy of Orthodox Christianity but accepted key points of Catholic doctrine, including the authority of the pope. Priests of the Jesuit order, dispatched by the Austrian court, devised the Uniate Church as a means of luring Transylvania's Romanians into the Catholic fold and so increasing its numbers, since most Lutherans and Calvinists strenuously resisted reconversion.

In return for becoming Uniates, the Jesuits offered Orthodox clergy exemption from serfdom and increased social status, although the Habsburgs did not go so far as to make the new church one of the four "received" religions. However, the development of the Uniate Church ultimately had the unintended effect of sparking a renewal of Romanian national consciousness. Young Uniate clerics were sent to Rome for education, where they saw Trajan's Column and became aware of the classical Roman and Dacian roots of their culture. They brought that knowledge home with them, adapting the Latin alphabet to the Romanian language in place of the Slavic Cyrillic script and publishing the first grammars and prayer books in modern Romanian. The southern Transylvanian city of Blaj, seat of the Uniate Church, became the hub of this cultural renaissance.

Emperor Joseph II (1780–90), an "enlightened despot," initiated a program of moderate reform throughout the Habsburg Empire to improve the lives of the serfs and preempt revolutions from below. He also decreed that German was to be the official language. These steps backfired in Transylvania, where the peasants rose up in an unsuccessful rebellion and Magyars began calling for the union of Transylvania and Hungary and the "Magyarization" of Romanian and other non-Hungarian peoples.

The situation came to a head when liberal and nationalist revolutions erupted across Europe in 1848. Hungary joined the revolt, abolishing serfdom and declaring the unification of Hungary and Transylvania. This touched off a bloody civil war in Transylvania, with Romanians and Saxons, aided by Austrian imperial troops, battling the Magyars. Eventually, with the aid of Russian forces, the revolution was crushed. Austria imposed a harsh military occupation on Transylvania, under which the Romanian population was no better off than before. Although there was a brief period of reform in 1863–65, by 1867 a weakened Habsburg Empire was forced to enter into a Dual Monarchy with Hungary. The result was that Transylvania was yet again united with Hungary, and the Romanians there faced another half-century of persecution at the hands of the Magyars.

Phanariot Rule and the Russian Occupations

From the beginning of the 18th century onward, the history of Walachia and Moldavia was at least as tumultuous as that of Transylvania. The era was primarily defined by the growing conflict between the Russian and Ottoman empires, in which the two Romanian principalities became a constant battleground.

Under Czar Peter the Great (1696–1725), the expanding Russian Empire had succeeded Poland as the most influential power in Eastern Europe. Peter proclaimed himself the champion of his fellow Orthodox Christians living under the Turkish yoke, and in 1711 he attempted to liberate Moldavia. The military bid failed, and the Ottomans, alarmed by the support shown by the Romanian princes for the Russian invasion, instituted what became known as the "Phanariot" system.

The Phanariots were Byzantines, aristocratic Greeks from Constantinople's Phanar, or lighthouse, district. No longer trusting the native Romanian nobles to be sufficiently pliant, the Sublime Porte henceforth appointed only Phanariots to be princes of Walachia and Moldavia. In exchange for their absolute loyalty to the sultan, the Phanariots were encouraged to take economic exploitation of their subjects to a new level, wringing as much wealth from the land and people as possible.

The new system resulted in widespread corruption and heightened economic misery. While the princes and boyars lived in relative luxury, the peasants and even most of the townspeople remained mired in primitive living conditions. An English traveler passing through Walachia in 1747 painted an unflattering portrait of its capital city: "Bucharest is a large straggling town of a very peculiar make, the outward parts very mean, consisting of houses, the greater part of which is underground like our cellars, and covered over at the top with straw or bark of trees."[5]

Most of all, it was a period characterized by a succession of wars, invasions, broken treaties, and diplomatic intrigues. Between 1711 and 1856, at least eight wars were waged on Romanian soil involving Russia, Austria, and the Turks. Aside from the vast human and material losses, these conflicts also resulted in various territorial maimings of Walachia and Moldavia.

Russia invaded the principalities in 1739, 1769, 1787, 1806, 1828, 1848, and 1853, occupying them as protectorates for long periods while gaining greater concessions from the weakening Turks and increased authority over internal Romanian affairs. While initially welcoming them as liberators, Romanians eventually came to see the Russians as just another foreign conqueror, and developed a strong distrust of their giant eastern neighbor that only deepened in the 20th century.

Phanariot rule came to an abrupt end in 1821 after an abortive anti-Ottoman rebellion by Greek nationalists led by Alexander Ypsilanti, son of a Phanariot prince and a general in the Russian army. He and his men seized control of Moldavia, while Tudor Vladimirescu, a Romanian whose military skills had allowed him to rise from peasant to boyar rank, led an anti-Phanariot revolt in Walachia. After their initial successes, the two men quarreled, the Greeks murdered Vladimirescu, and the Turks (with Russia's approval) proceeded to crush Ypsilanti's insurgency. The Sublime Porte, now fearing the loyalty of its Greek subjects, returned to its old practice of appointing native Romanians as princes.

The Union of Moldavia and Walachia

Ironically, for all the difficulties caused by Russia's interventions, it was a Russian general who helped lay the groundwork for the eventual unification of Moldavia and Walachia. Count Pavel Kiselev, who administered the two territories during Russia's 1829–34 occupation, was something of a liberal schooled in the ideals of French Enlightenment tradition. During his tenure, he organized the principalities' first modern police force, medical service, and grain reserves. Conditions in the cities gradually improved, although life in the countryside remained mostly miserable. A traveler in Walachia in 1835 reported not seeing "either manor house, bridge, windmills, or inn, or furniture or utensils in the peasant huts."[6]

Most importantly, Kiselev oversaw the promulgation of the Reglement Organique (Organic Regulations, or Constitution), a system of fundamental laws that provided for princes to be chosen by an elected assembly of boyars and clergy. It also reformed the judiciary and set up the first public education system. Although it included some regressive economic provisions—reducing peasant mobility and increasing peasant obligations to the boyars—the main benefit of the Reglement Organique was to provide both Walachia and Moldavia with identical systems of government, even while they remained separate political entities.

The final spur for unification came from the European-wide revolutions of 1848. Inspired by the uprising in Transylvania, radical Romanian nationalists also rose up in Moldavia and Walachia, seeking independence from foreign domination. The conservative Russian and Ottoman empires acted together to snuff out the rebellions, and many of the radicals fled to France as political refugees.

Many of these youthful émigrés had been educated in Paris and were welcomed back as revolutionary heroes. This attitude was epitomized by a famous remark made at the time by a woman of Parisian high society: "So young and already Moldo-Walachian!"[7] Similarly, a historian drew this romantic picture of the typical Romanian émigré:

> The exile was a young man with long hair, flashing eyes, with a large Carbonari hat, high collar with a scarf wound around it up to his ears and who had only to roll up his sleeves to show the wounds Tyranny had inflicted on him. He was loaded with news sheets, brochures and proclamations. Politicians bowed before an outlaw.[8]

The Russians themselves set the stage for Romanian independence in 1853 when, badly misjudging the international climate, they invaded the principalities yet one more time. This action precipitated the Crimean War, which saw Russia defeated in its attempt to seize territory from the declining Ottoman Empire. The Turks were backed by Britain, France,

Austria, and other European powers, which wanted to preserve the balance of power in the region.

Austrian and Turkish troops forced Russia to withdraw from Moldavia and Walachia. Under the 1856 Treaty of Paris, a joint European guarantee replaced the Russian protectorate, and it was agreed that no power was to enjoy "exclusive protection" of the principalities, although the Turks continued to exercise nominal sovereignty. In addition, the treaty freed navigation on the Danube and compelled Russia to return a section of southern Bessarabia, including control of the Danube's mouth, to Moldavia.

These events prompted an active movement by Romanian nationalists for the unification of Walachia and Moldavia. The campaign had the backing of the French government of Napoleon III, thanks to the influence of the Romanian émigrés in Paris. The Ottomans, Austria, and Britain were opposed; Russia proposed to allow the Romanians themselves to vote on the issue. A referendum was held in 1857 in which the unionists lost, but the rigging of the election by the Turks (allegedly with British connivance) was so blatant that it prompted an international crisis.

A new vote resulted in a large majority of delegates in favor of unification. The unionists followed up by issuing a call for a constitutional government to be headed by a foreign prince who would rule over both principalities. But the international community still favored caution, and a conference in Paris in 1858 asserted that Moldavia and Walachia should retain separate governments under loose Turkish control. On the other hand, the conference also named the two states the "United Principalities" (while resisting use of the name "Romania") and said they could share a common currency and legal system.

Finally, the Romanian nationalists came up with a clever solution to overcome the imposed political division: In January 1859 the separate assemblies in Iasi, Moldavia, and Bucharest, Walachia, elected the same man—Alexandru Ioan Cuza, liberal son of a Moldavian boyar—as the governor of their respective principalities. Caught by surprise and distracted by a military crisis in Italy, Europe's leading powers accepted the de facto unification and allowed Cuza to become prince.

Further discussions led to formal European and Ottoman recognition of the union of Walachia and Moldavia in 1861. Cuza, who had been shuttling between the assemblies and ministries in Bucharest and Iasi for the past two years, officially established the nation's capital at Bucharest, the country's largest city. On November 11, 1861, he was able to proclaim: "The Union has been accomplished, the Romanian nation has been founded. As your elected representative, I present you today one single Romania."[9] The following month, with what later proved to be considerable foresight, he remarked, "I fear you will not be satisfied with me for long."[10]

It took a grudging Europe some 15 years to adopt the name Romania for the new state, and by then Cuza himself was long gone from the scene.

NOTES

1. Andrei Otetea, ed., *The History of the Romanian People*, p. 195.
2. Bram Stoker, *Dracula*, p. 2 (Bantam Classic edition, 1981).
3. Otetea, op. cit., p. 201.
4. Denise Basdevant, *Against Tide and Tempest*, p. 23.
5. Julian Hale, *The Land and People of Romania*, p. 37.
6. Basdevant, op. cit., p. 46.
7. Ibid, p. 51.
8. Ibid.
9. Ibid, p. 60.
10. Edward Behr, *Kiss the Hand You Cannot Bite*, p. 35.

3

From the Late 19ᵗʰ Century through the World Wars

---

*S*hortly after the official unification of Moldavia and Walachia in 1861, Prince Alexandru Cuza (1859–66) began a bold program of domestic reform. His efforts surprised some observers, as he had been elected as a compromise candidate and had not had a particularly distinguished political career up to that point.

In the face of close international attention, he had to carry out a careful balancing act. The Ottoman Empire regularly threatened to reoccupy the principalities, to which menacing the Russians responded by backing a Moldavian separatist movement. The British worried about anything that might give the Russians an excuse to expand their influence. And the Austrians feared that the new state would ignite Romanian nationalist fervor in Transylvania and Bukovina.

Fortunately for Cuza, the actions of Turkey, Russia, and Britain tended to offset each other, while Austria was preoccupied with the crisis of Italian independence. But most important of all was the critical diplomatic and military support given to Romania by the French government of Napoleon III. Appreciating this, Cuza wrote to his foreign envoys: "Do not let France cool toward us at any price, because, in my opinion, she is the only power on whom we can really count."[1]

Cuza had less success in balancing domestic objections to his rule. Radical elements of the Liberal Party faulted him for not repudiating Ottoman influence and for not working harder to reunite Romania with its neighboring countrymen still living under foreign domination. At the other end of the political spectrum, the Conservative Party, controlled largely by the boyar class of rich landlords, was alienated by his efforts to purge Romania of its remaining vestiges of feudalism.

To outflank his political opponents, Cuza in 1864 dissolved the legislative assembly and took his case directly to the people in a national referendum. Winning a vote of confidence from the peasant majority, he passed a new electoral law granting universal suffrage (voting rights), establishing a more modern legislature, and, following the example of Napoleon III, giving himself essentially dictatorial powers to carry out his reform program.

Cuza rewarded the peasants with an agrarian law that formally abolished serfdom, tithes (enforced payments to landlords), and forced labor. The law also allowed peasants to own land, allotting 2 million hectares (5 million acres) to 400,000 peasants. But in part because of opposition by the boyars, the new plots were too expensive for most peasants and too small to be farmed for a profit. As a result, economic conditions for many people in rural areas actually worsened.

Cuza also carried out other, less controversial reforms. These included new criminal and civil codes modeled on the French legal system, an improved road system, the establishment of compulsory, free elementary education, and the founding of universities in Iasi and Bucharest.

Eventually, Cuza's missteps antagonized the ordinary people, who joined with the political elite in opposition. Popular anger mounted over the regime's economic mismanagement and corruption, and over Cuza's increasingly dictatorial and "regal" behavior, along with scandals in his personal life. (According to one rumor, he was attempting to arrange for one of his mistress's sons to succeed him on the throne.)

After the government's brutal suppression of a riot in Bucharest, the Liberals and Conservatives joined together in February 1866 to oust the first ruler of modern Romania. Army officers woke Cuza and his mistress in the palace, forced the prince to sign papers of abdication, and escorted him out of the country.

King Carol I

With the departure of Cuza, the government announced a regency pending the election of a foreign prince, as the unionists had long sought. (Rule by a foreign-born monarch would avoid charges of favoritism toward either Moldavia or Walachia.) After shopping around through the royal houses of Europe, Liberal Party leader Ion Bratianu nominated Prince Charles of southern Germany's Hohenzollern-Sigmaringen family, a choice backed by France's Napoleon III and Prussian Premier Otto von Bismarck. The selection of the 27-year-old prince was approved in a Romanian referendum, and he was formally invited to assume the throne.

Charles—Karl in German or Carol in Romanian, as he was subsequently known—feared being stopped along the way if he traveled openly via Russia or Austria, which was on the verge of war with Prussia. So he made the journey to Romania disguised as a common salesman, traveling under a false passport by second-class rail and steamboat through Austrian territory, reaching Bucharest in May 1866. He would rule the country until his death in 1914.

Upon arriving in his new home, Carol was apparently shocked by its backward state. At one point he asked where he was and was told he had reached the royal palace. "Looking at the building and thinking he had not heard correctly, [Carol] asked, '*Where* is the Palace?' His informant could only point in embarrassment to the low building that looked out on an undistinguished guardhouse and gypsy camp, with its group of pigs wallowing in the mud."[2]

During his reign, Carol tried to provide the country with a modern administration, despite facing a succession of Liberal and Conservative governments that rose and fell in elections that were often corrupt. Among his major contributions were presiding over the building of the country's first railroad system and the modernization of Romania's armed forces, undertaken with the aid of Prussian advisers. But in a country overwhelmingly sympathetic to France, Carol also found himself enduring opposition and insults due to his own Prussian origins. The atmosphere reached crisis proportions during the Franco-Prussian War of 1870–71 (in which France was soundly defeated), and Carol came close to abdicating.

During the 1877–78 Russo-Turkish War, the Romanian parliament voted to support what it perceived as the lesser of two evils and came out on the side of Russia. It declared Romania to be finally and permanently free of Ottoman sovereignty and allowed Russian forces to pass through Romanian territory to attack the Turks. When Russian troops became trapped south of the Danube at Plevna (in present-day Bulgaria), the Romanian army, personally led by Prince Carol, came to their rescue and helped rout the Turks.

Despite Romania's crucial contribution to their victory, the Russians refused to let Romania participate in the 1878 Congress of Berlin that settled the issues resulting from the war. In the end, Romania was forced to accept Russia's annexation of southern Bessarabia from Moldavia, while in return it gained control over northern Dobruja, which included the Danube delta. Europe agreed to recognize Romania's formal and complete independence, in exchange for two main conditions: one, that it consent to the territorial deal with Russia, and two, that it guarantee equality of civil, political, and religious rights. The last condition was aimed at forcing Romania to repeal its laws discriminating against Jews.

Jews first began immigrating to Romania in substantial numbers after 1829. From 1859 to 1899, the number of Jews in Moldavia increased from about 118,000 to 200,000, while in Walachia it grew from 9,000 to 68,000. (In Iasi, the Moldavian capital, about half the population was Jewish.) Fearing their expertise in financial and business matters—areas that most Romanians remained ignorant of—the government passed laws preventing Jews from owning land or even becoming innkeepers. An article in

A statue of King Carol I (1866–1914), Romania's most beloved modern monarch, stands outside Peles Castle in Sinaia. (Romanian Cultural Center)

CAROL I
PRIMUL REGE AL
ROMANIEI
1866-1914

the new constitution specifically forbade them from holding the civil and political rights of Romanian citizens.

This official anti-Semitism, which was to plague Romania over the course of the next century, was widely shared at all levels of Romanian society. The peasantry came to resent the Jewish role as moneylenders (a position they filled by default, as Romanian banks showed no interest in lending to the poor) and as stewards of large rural estates, which they managed on behalf of absentee landlords. The growing middle class viewed the Jews as direct competitors. And members of the rich landlord class that dominated the government, who themselves owed large sums to Jewish lenders, feared that if Jews were granted equal rights they would be in a position to simply buy out their clients.

And so, in times of trouble, the Jewish minority became a scapegoat for the country's problems. In one historian's words, "The Romanians learned to curse the Turk, the Russian, the Hungarian . . . and to beat the Jew."[3]

For all these reasons, Romania at first resisted the demands of the Congress of Berlin, as debate raged in the parliament and anti-Jewish protests erupted in the streets. But the European powers held firm, and eventually the government agreed to repeal most of the anti-Jewish statutes, although the changes left numerous loopholes that allowed continued discrimination. Nevertheless, the Great Powers signaled their satisfaction with the reforms, and in early 1881 they officially recognized Romania's independence.

In March 1881, the country's parliament proclaimed the "Kingdom of Romania." On May 22, amid much solemn fanfare in Bucharest's cathedral, Prince Carol was invested as King Carol I. The crown placed on his head at the ceremony had been fashioned from the metal of a Turkish cannon captured at the pivotal battle of Plevna.

The coronation was an expensive, glittering affair, and in some ways it showed how far the country had come in the 15 years since Carol arrived and found pigs rooting outside his "palace." (Carol responded over the years of his reign with a succession of royal building projects, erecting expensive palaces that were "turreted, pinnacled and ornamented down to the last square meter."[4])

But not all the changes were so superficial. Romania borrowed heavily from abroad (primarily from Germany) to finance economic development, and by the end of the 19th century the country had nearly 9,000 miles of roadway and 2,000 miles of railroad (14,000 kilometers and 3,100 kilometers, respectively). Walachia began pumping petroleum from its own wells, and public schools were built throughout the country. Between 1870 and 1898, the kingdom's foreign trade more than tripled.

Peasant Revolt and the Balkan Wars

Most of this economic development, however, benefited only Romania's wealthy classes, while the vast majority of the country's peasantry continued to labor in debt and peonage. A peasant uprising in Walachia after the harsh winter of 1887–88 resulted in the government's passage of an agrarian reform act that proved as inadequate as those before it. The pressure in the countryside built up steadily over the next two decades until it exploded with unprecedented ferocity in 1907.

The peasant revolt that erupted in Moldavia in March of that year began as an anti-Semitic pogrom, or organized massacre, with mobs attacking Jewish middlemen. It rapidly spread through much of the country and took on the characteristics of full-fledged class warfare as the enraged peasantry sacked large rural estates, burned the mansions of the rich, and finally tried to march on Bucharest. The government declared a state of siege and brought out the army, which suppressed the revolt with brutal efficiency. The rebels, armed only with primitive weapons, stood no chance against modern firearms, and at least 11,000 peasants were killed.

Romania's political and economic elite was chilled by the paroxysm of violence, and under the leadership of the Liberal Party a land reform program more thorough than any previous program was enacted. It established a minimum wage for agricultural laborers, set a maximum rent that could be charged to peasants leasing land, created rural banks, and dispersed some 4 million hectares (10 million acres) to needy peasants. Although it did not attack the root causes of the land conflict, the program was a positive step that temporarily helped reduce social tensions.

As a small, vulnerable state in a volatile region, Romania cast about for allies to help protect it against potential enemies. In 1883, King Carol had signed a secret treaty of alliance with Germany and Austria-Hungary—the so-called Central Powers. The treaty was a product of Romania's abiding mistrust of Russia, combined with the weakened power of France, Romania's traditional ally, and Carol's predilection toward his own German heritage.

The treaty was so secret that the only copy of it was kept locked inside the king's personal safe in the mountain castle that served as his summer retreat. The parliament had no idea of its existence. In some Romanian governments, Carol was the *only* person who was aware of the vital document. When the treaty came up for renewal in later years, certain key ministers were "brought into the loop."

One reason for the secrecy was to avoid antagonizing Britain, France, and Russia, who later joined together to form the Triple Entente, set up to counter the Central Powers. But a more important one was to avoid outraging the Romanian people themselves. It was clear to all concerned that Romanians would be horrified to discover they were formally allied with Austria-Hungary, the power that occupied Bukovina and Transylvania.

The issue was particularly sensitive because, during the period from 1879 to 1910, the Hungarian authorities enacted increasingly draconian laws to oppress non-Magyar nationalities in Transylvania. The use of the Hungarian language was mandated in schools, a campaign was launched to Magyarize family names, and when the Romanian masses tried to protest and organize politically, they were arrested and their rights of assembly were abolished. All of this sparked public outrage in Romania, along with growing calls for unification with Transylvania.

The international situation became almost impossibly complicated in 1912–13, the period of the two Balkan Wars. Austria-Hungary was becoming extremely concerned with the threat posed by Serbia, and began to see Bulgaria as a potential ally. This worried Romania, which had territorial conflicts with Bulgaria. Then, in the First Balkan War of October 1912, Bulgaria joined with Serbia, Montenegro, and Greece to attack the waning Ottoman Empire, with the tacit approval of Russia. Romania sat on the sidelines as the Balkan states dealt the Turks a serious defeat. In the negotiations that followed, Romania and Bulgaria quarreled bitterly.

The Second Balkan War erupted in June 1913 when Bulgaria, emboldened by its successes, turned on its former allies and attacked Serbia and Greece. In a bizarre shift of alliances, this time both Romania and Turkey joined in the fighting against Bulgaria, which had seriously overestimated its own strength. The brief war ended with Romania in control of the southern Dobruja region that had previously been part of Bulgaria. But the Balkans remained dangerous, and the stage was now set for the cataclysmic struggle initially called the Great War, although it ultimately became known as World War I.

World War I and Greater Romania

On June 28, 1914, a Bosnian Serb terrorist assassinated Austria's Archduke Franz Ferdinand in the Bosnian capital of Sarajevo, touching off a continent-wide conflict. Ferdinand, the heir to the Habsburg throne, was the most prominent advocate in Austria-Hungary of the rights of Transylvania's Romanians. Austria issued a harsh ultimatum to Serbia, which was allied with Russia and France, that was tantamount to a declaration of war.

Initially, King Carol felt that since Austria had provoked Serbia with its ultimatum, the circumstances did not obligate Romania to honor its secret treaty with the Central Powers. But he swiftly became squeezed by both sides: The Central Powers appealed to his German heritage and promised that Romania would win back Bessarabia if it joined in the coming war against Russia. Moscow, in turn, raised the prospect that Romania could gain control of Transylvania if it joined the Triple Entente.

On August 3, 1914, as war broke out across Europe, a dramatic meeting of the Romanian Crown Council (consisting of both government and opposition party leaders) was held at the king's Carpathian palace in Sinaia. Carol forcefully called for siding with the Central Powers. But the council—many of whose members had learned about the king's secret, unconstitutional treaty for the first time—voted, with the exception of one minister, to remain neutral. They knew the Romanian people would not join any war alongside their Hungarian enemy and against France, their longtime friend.

"You cannot imagine," the king remarked after the meeting, "how bitter it is to find oneself isolated in a country of which one is not a native."[5]

A disconsolate Carol died in his sleep on October 10, 1914, without having left a direct heir. Following arrangements made 25 years before, he was succeeded on the throne by his nephew, Ferdinand I (1914–27). Ferdinand was a considerably weaker and less politically astute ruler than his uncle. If it had not been for the traumatic outbreak of war, Carol's passing would have occasioned a much more emotional outburst of national mourning in Romania, for he had presided over the most peaceful and prosperous 48-year era in his adopted country's history.

Romania clung to its neutrality for the first two years of the war, and even profited handsomely by it, selling grain, oil, and other goods to both sides at inflated prices. Meanwhile, Bucharest engaged in extensive diplomatic haggling with both the Central Powers and the Triple Entente, seeking the best possible territorial deal before it entered the conflict on one side or the other. Ferdinand's wife, Queen Marie, was a member of both the British and Russian royal families and used her contacts to pass Romania's demands along to both of their governments.

In the summer of 1916 the battlefield situation seemed to be tipping toward the Entente, which finally agreed to Romania's conditions: that it would ultimately gain control of Transylvania, Bukovina, and the Banat from Austria-Hungary and perhaps even Bessarabia from Russia. The Crown Council met again on August 27, 1916, and declared war on Germany and Austria-Hungary. King Ferdinand, however, was traumatized by having to forsake his German roots. According to a French envoy, he appeared "ravaged by an interior struggle, his voice cut with sobs, his hands trembling."[6]

The good news was that Romania had backed what ultimately proved to be the winning side in World War I. The bad news—typical of the country's tortured history—was that it would suffer terribly before finally reaping its reward. Romania's military establishment, previously dependent on German arms and advisers, was thoroughly unprepared for modern war. Britain and France initially could not deliver on their promises of military aid, and the Russian troops that entered Romania to lend support proved to be worse than useless, leaving all the hard fighting to their Romanian "allies."

The Romanian army invaded Transylvania, but was quickly driven back by German and Austrian forces, while the combined armies of Germany, Bulgaria, and Turkey counterattacked from the south. Bucharest and the rest of Walachia came under occupation as the Romanian government retreated to Moldavia. There, with the help of a French military mission, a reorganized Romanian army scored some successes on the battlefield. But with the triumph of the Bolshevik Revolution against Russia's provisional government in November 1917, Russia was transformed from a weak ally into an actively hostile power as the Bolsheviks made peace with Germany and withdrew from the war.

Now completely isolated, Romania sued for peace with the Central Powers. The terms were harsh: It ceded most of Transylvania to Hungary and Dobruja to Bulgaria, and was forced to sign its agricultural and oil wealth over to Germany while paying reparations to a German occupation army even as thousands of Romanians were dying from famine and disease. By the end of the war, Romania had suffered more than 800,000 military and civilian dead, a huge total for such a small country. The only positive development was that Romania gained control of Bessarabia from Russia.

But by the middle of 1918, aided by the American entry into the war against Germany, the military tide turned against the Central Powers. In November Romania again declared war on Germany, and its army—which had not been demobilized—reoccupied Walachia and most of Transylvania. Nationalist assemblies in Transylvania, Bukovina, and Bessarabia voted for union with their Romanian motherland. In peace treaties signed in 1919 and 1920, the international community sanctioned virtually all of Romania's territorial claims, granting it sovereignty over Bessarabia, Bukovina, Transylvania, and Dobruja, and partitioning control of the Banat region between Romania and Serbia. Thus was Greater Romania born.

But the fighting was not quite over. In mid-1919, in response to provocations by a Communist regime, led by Bela Kun, that briefly took power in Hungary, the Romanian army invaded Hungary and occupied its capital, Budapest. Taking what they saw as justified revenge for the looting of Romania during the war, the Romanian forces thoroughly plundered their historic enemy's territory. When they withdrew from Budapest in early 1920, under pressure from the Western Allies, the Romanians took with them practically everything of value they could transport: railroad cars and locomotives, trucks, factory equipment, and food. After centuries of Hungarian domination over Romanians, this reversal of fortune further hardened attitudes between the two nations.

The Inter-War Years

Virtually overnight, Romania had more than doubled both its prewar population (from 7.5 million to 16 million) and territory (from about 86,000 sq. mi. to 185,000 sq. mi. [138,000 to 295,000 sq. km.]). Although the expanded borders realized the age-old dream of uniting virtually all Romanians in one single state, they also brought in a much greater number of restive, non-Romanian nationalities. Whereas Romanians had made up 92 percent of the population in the old kingdom, that figure dropped to 70 percent in Greater Romania.

To ward off the prospect of revolution, and to keep patriotic promises made to the peasantry by King Ferdinand during the war, Romania's postwar governments enacted a series of political and social reforms. A new constitution in 1923 established Romania as a modern parliamentary monarchy with a highly centralized administration. Although the charter included a liberal list of guaranteed civil and political rights (such as universal male suffrage and citizenship for Jews), their subsequent enforcement was often more theoretical than real.

New agrarian laws passed between 1917 and 1921 substantially altered the country's system of land distribution. Huge swaths of land belonging to the boyars, the church, the Crown, and absentee landlords were sold to peasants to the point where small farmers with plots of 10 hectares (25 acres) or less now controlled more than 60 percent of the tilled land. But, as in previous land reform schemes, the small size of the plots—combined with corruption, lawsuits, insufficient rural credit, and inadequate farming equipment—meant that most peasants were still unable to escape their age-old cycle of poverty.

Although it remained a primarily agrarian country, Romania had considerable success in modernizing its industry during this period. Its industrial output doubled between 1923 and 1938, and by the mid-1930s it ranked second in Europe and seventh in the world in petroleum production. Its per capita income in 1938 was $94 (as compared to $81 in Portugal and $76 in Greece), although most of the wealth remained in the hands of the elite.

On the political scene, the old Conservative Party had been demolished by both the war, when it backed Germany, and the subsequent land reform, which lessened the power of its boyar patrons. Its traditional opponent, the Liberal Party, had by now strayed far from its populist 19th-century roots and was dominated by the country's industrial and financial classes. Its place on the political left was taken by the National Party (the major Romanian party in prewar Transylvania), which joined in 1926 with the old kingdom's Peasant Party to form the National Peasant Party. The Liberals retained power through mostly crooked elections from 1922 to 1928, while the National Peasant Party controlled the government, with one interruption, from 1928 to 1933.

A crisis in the royal family deepened Romania's continuing political turmoil. Crown Prince Carol II, Ferdinand's son and heir, was a notorious womanizer who married a Greek princess in 1921 but then promptly began a long-term affair with a divorced Jewish stenographer named Elena (Magda) Lupescu. The highly publicized scandal made Romania the butt of jokes all over Europe. When King Ferdinand demanded his son break off the affair, Carol instead abdicated his right of succession and went into exile in Paris with Lupescu. Ferdinand died on July 19, 1927, and Carol's six-year-old son Michael was named king while a regency council ruled in his name.

Public dissatisfaction with the regency mounted when Romania was plunged into economic crisis by the Great Depression, the global economic crash that began in 1929. National Party Premier Iuliu Maniu agreed to allow Carol to return in 1930 if he broke off his affair, reconciled with his wife (they had been divorced in 1928), and agreed to rule initially only as co-regent, not king. Carol promptly broke all his promises, bringing Lupescu with him and allowing parliament to proclaim him King Carol II (1930–40). Maniu resigned in disgust. "Clever, tireless and quite without scruples he was exactly the king Romania did not need, for his own bad qualities matched and then magnified those of his country," as one modern writer has noted.[7]

In the years that followed, Carol gradually revealed himself to be more of a royal dictator than a democratic monarch. To aid his consolidation of power, he forged informal and ambiguous links with the Iron Guard, an extreme nationalist, far-right, anti-Semitic and anticommunist—that is to say, Fascist—group founded in the 1920s by Corneliu Zelea Codreanu. Codreanu was subsidized by Romanian industrialists who opposed the multiparty political system. The Iron Guard also received backing from abroad: first from the Fascist Party of Italian dictator Benito Mussolini and later from the Nazi Party of German dictator Adolf Hitler.

The Guard's official name was the Legion of the Archangel Michael, and its fanatical members were known as legionnaires. Jackbooted and wearing green shirts with little bags of "sacred" Romanian soil hanging from their necks, they assaulted leftists and Jews and engaged in political terrorism, assassinating premiers in 1933 and 1939. Poor, angry peasants flocked to the Iron Guard's banner, swelling its ranks until it became the largest Fascist party in the Balkans.

Carol eventually felt threatened by the Guard's power, and was shocked when its candidates won major victories in the 1937 elections. In 1938, the king cracked down on the legionnaires, arresting thousands of them. Codreanu and 13 other senior leaders were gunned down in prison "while trying to escape," although reportedly they were executed on Carol's orders. The king also suspended the constitution and proclaimed a royal dictatorship, ruling through the semi-Fascist "Front of National Renaissance" that he founded as a less extreme alternative to the Iron Guard.

Meanwhile, war again threatened Europe. Earlier, Romania had tried to design a system of international alliances to protect the gains it had made in World War I. In the 1920s, it had joined in a pro-French, anti-German pact with Czechoslovakia and Yugoslavia (two states that had emerged from the collapse of the Habsburg Empire) known as the Little Entente. In the early 1930s, Romania added an alliance with Greece, Turkey, and Yugoslavia—the Balkan Entente, aimed mainly against Bulgaria.

Romania's confidence in its security net began to wane throughout the 1930s, as fascism increased its grip, and the growing might of Nazi Germany asserted itself on the world stage. Germany deliberately increased its influence in Romania, paying higher prices for its grain and oil, to the point where it accounted for half of Romania's total imports and exports. Hitler knew that Romania's agricultural and petroleum resources would be crucial to the German war machine in the coming war in Eastern Europe and Russia.

In September 1938, France and Britain signed the fateful Munich Agreement with Germany that allowed Hitler to carve up Czechoslovakia, making the Little Entente a dead letter. Feeling abandoned by her Western allies, Romania was forced to accommodate itself to German demands. In March 1939 the two countries signed a 10-year treaty of economic collaboration granting Germany extensive and exclusive rights to exploit Romania's natural resources.

World War II

In August 1939, Hitler signed a nonaggression pact with Soviet dictator Josef Stalin, leaving Romania caught between the German and Russian juggernauts. The treaty freed Hitler to launch his invasion of Poland in September, starting World War II. Romania granted refuge and transit rights to the fleeing remnants of Poland's government and armed forces. But, although Britain and France had previously guaranteed the independence of Romania, their quick defeats in the West at the hands of the Nazis made that bold pledge a hollow echo. British forces retreated to their home islands, and France surrendered in June 1940.

Unknown to Romania, the Nazi-Soviet pact had included a secret clause giving Moscow a free hand to reclaim Bessarabia. On June 26, 1940, the Soviets gave Romania a 24-hour ultimatum to turn over not only Bessarabia but also northern Bukovina, a region that had never been under Russian control. King Carol II, while trying to stay neutral in the conflict, was left with no choice but to give in to the Soviet demands. In August, under German, Soviet, and Italian pressure, Romania was forced to return southern Dobruja to Bulgaria and northern Transylvania to Hungary. Within three months, Greater Romania was swiftly dismembered, losing a third of its national territory and 4 million of its citizens.

This national humiliation proved to be the end for Carol. In a last-ditch effort to retain power, he named pro-legionnaire Marshal Ion Antonescu premier. But Antonescu, in league with the major political parties, army officers, and the Iron Guard, and with the full backing of Nazi Germany,

Advance troops of the Soviet Red Army are "welcomed" by Romanian civilians in northern Bukovina in July 1940. (AP/Wide World Photos)

November 1940: A German army commission arrives in Bucharest to supervise the "training" of Romania's military. A Romanian honor guard stands at right. (AP/Wide World Photos)

forced Carol to abdicate on September 6, 1940. He fled into exile with Lupescu, his mistress, leaving his now 19-year-old son, Michael V (1940–47), to take the throne.

Antonescu assumed the grandiose title of Conducator, or leader (analogous to Hitler's Führer), ignored King Michael, and ruled as a military dictator in uneasy alliance with the Iron Guard. Beginning in October, German troops began moving into Romania, supposedly to "train" its armed forces and protect its vital oil industry. In reality, it was an army of occupation that eventually numbered up to one million men. On November 23, 1940, Romania officially joined the Nazi-led Axis Powers.

This period represented the high-water mark of the Iron Guard, which continued to function more as a macabre cult than a political movement.

Nevertheless, it was tolerated by Antonescu and the cowed political elite. "In Legionnaire, bourgeois, nationalist Romania I saw the demon of sadism and stubborn stupidity incarnate before me," remarked playwright Eugène Ionesco.[8]

In November 1940, Antonescu and the army stood by while the legionnaires launched a reign of terror, murdering Jews, kidnapping and killing Nicolae Iorga, a noted historian and one-time premier, and slaughtering 64 prominent members of King Carol's regime in Bucharest's central prison in revenge for the death of Codreanu. Finally, Germany decided that its fellow Fascists had gone too far—after having served the Nazis' ulterior purpose of destabilizing Romania—and German and Romanian troops began rounding up the gangs of thugs. "I don't need fanatics, I need a healthy Romanian army," Hitler told Antonescu.[9]

When Antonescu moved against the Iron Guard's leadership in January 1941, purging his regime of its members, the legionnaires staged an open rebellion aimed at seizing power for themselves. After they carried out a particularly ghastly massacre and mutilation of nearly 200 Jewish civilians in a slaughterhouse, German and Romanian soldiers cracked down hard and crushed the Iron Guard after several weeks of fighting.

On June 22, 1941, Germany broke its pact with Moscow and launched a lightning invasion of the Soviet Union across a broad front in Eastern Europe. German and Romanian armies attacked from the southwest and, in short order, Romania gained back northern Bukovina and Bessarabia from Soviet control. Many prudent Romanians felt they should have stopped there and left further conquests to the Germans. But with Antonescu calling for a "holy war" against communism, Romanian troops advanced across the Dniester River into the Ukraine with their German allies, seizing the Black Sea ports of Odessa and Sevastopol.

According to Grigore Gafencu, an intellectual Romanian statesman of the period, his country "was carried along in the vortex of the war, chained to a cause which was beyond her interest, fearing her ally as much as her adversary and the peace of tomorrow as much as the war of today."[10]

Romania contributed more combat troops to the German war effort than all of the other Nazi allies combined. In part, it hoped to curry Hitler's favor so that Romania would win back northern Transylvania from Hungary after the war, which was expected to end in a quick victory for the Axis Powers. But the German and Romanian columns became stalled on the frozen Russian steppes as one bitter winter passed, and then another. Finally, the turning point of the war was reached in the epic battle of Stalingrad, when the Soviet Red Army counterattacked and, in February 1943, totally destroyed the German and Romanian armies besieging the city.

It became increasingly clear that Germany would eventually lose the war. From the middle of 1943 on, acting separately, both the Antonescu regime and the leaders of Romania's opposition parties initiated secret negotiations with the Western Allies, even as British and American bombers were pounding Romanian factories and the oil fields at Ploiesti. Romania was ready to surrender to Anglo-American forces to avoid Soviet occupation, but the Western powers were unwilling to agree to a peace that excluded their Soviet ally.

In August 1944, the Red Army crossed into Moldavia. On August 23, King Michael, acting in concert with a coalition of opposition politicians, army officers, and Communist militiamen, staged a coup. Michael personally arrested Antonescu, announced the formation of a government of national unity, declared peace with the Allies, and demanded the withdrawal of German troops from Romania. The next day the German units, under orders from an enraged Hitler, began a savage bombardment of Bucharest in a failed attempt to crush the coup.

Soviet troops occupied Bucharest a week after Michael staged his patriotic putsch. They would subsequently serve as the shield behind which the tiny Romanian Communist Party, founded in 1921, would rise up and seize absolute power. To cover up their embarrassing lack of underground activity against the Germans to that point, the Communists claimed to have played the predominant role in overthrowing Antonescu, although more objective observers agreed that most of the credit belonged to Michael. It was not the last time the Communists would rewrite Romania's history to suit their purposes.

On September 12, Romania signed a treaty in Moscow requiring it to cede Bessarabia and northern Bukovina back to the Soviet Union and pay stiff reparations. Meanwhile, the Romanian army threw itself into the war against its former German allies with great vigor. In the first phase of the war, against the Soviet Union, Romania had suffered several hundred thousand dead, missing, or captured (few prisoners returned alive from Soviet camps). In the last phase, fighting alongside the Red Army to liberate Hungary and Czechoslovakia, at least another 120,000 Romanians died. Altogether, Romania lost more men than the United States in all

The Romanian Holocaust

There were 800,000 Jews in Romania in 1939, the third largest Jewish population in Europe. By the end of the war, only 400,000 remained alive. Although the numbers killed were horrifying, France, for example, allowed an even larger percentage of Jews to be deported to their deaths, while the Romanian Holocaust did not approach the scale of the annihilation carried out by the Nazis in Poland. The Romanian authorities under Gen. Ion Antonescu resisted deporting "their" Jews to Nazi death camps. (However, Hungary's Nazi regime did deport or kill some 120,000 of Transylvania's 150,000 Jews in 1944.) Instead, Romanian soldiers, police, and Iron Guards initially murdered tens of thousands of Jews in vicious pogroms in Moldavia, Bukovina, and Bessarabia, as well as in the Ukrainian cities they conquered with their German allies, and later allowed hundreds of thousands of others to perish of disease and starvation.

But their crude methods were not as efficient as those perfected by the Germans, with their poison gas and crematoria. When told of the undisciplined massacre of 7,000 Jews carried out in a single night in June 1941 in Iasi, Moldavia, by Romanian soldiers and civilians, one Nazi official commented disdainfully: "Pogroms are a Slavic specialty. In all things, we Germans are guided by reason and method and not by bestial instincts; we always act scientifically . . . We use surgeons, not butchers."[11]

Labeling them all closet Bolsheviks (Communists), Antonescu's regime herded virtually the entire Jewish population of Bukovina and Bessarabia across the Dniester River into a desolate corner of the southwest Ukraine temporarily awarded to Romania by the Germans and dubbed "Transnistria." There, between 100,000 and 200,000 Jews were forced into concentration camps where up to three-quarters of them would die slowly of exposure, sickness, and hunger by the end of the war.

There was a ray of light amid the desolation, however. Siegfried Jagendorf, a Jewish engineer, persuaded the local Romanian authorities to allow him to repair a war-shattered foundry (ironworks factory) in the city of Moghilev. He recruited Jews as workers and devised projects to keep them alive and protect their wives, children, and the community's orphans. His heroic achievement, which ultimately saved up to 15,000 lives, bore a striking resemblance to the more famous effort of German industrialist Oskar Schindler, as chronicled in the book and movie *Schindler's List*.[12]

theaters of World War II, although it had only a small fraction of America's population.

NOTES

1. Denise Basdevant, *Against Tide and Tempest*, p. 62.
2. Hannah Pakula, *Queen Marie of Romania*, p. 36.
3. Siegfried Jagendorf, *Jagendorf's Foundry*, p. xix.
4. Pakula, op. cit., p. 39.
5. Edward Behr, *Kiss the Hand You Cannot Bite*, p. 43.
6. Ibid, p. 44.
7. Mark Frankland, *The Patriots' Revolution*, p. 8.
8. Norman Manea, *On Clowns: The Dictator and the Artist*, p. 3.
9. Jagendorf, op. cit., p. xxii.
10. Basdevant, op. cit., p. 104.
11. Jagendorf, op. cit., p. xxiv.
12. Ibid.

4

The Socialist Republic: Communism & Ceausescu

For the next 35 years, the history of Romania would, in essence, be the history of its Communist Party. This was a remarkable development for a party that, at the end of World War II, listed fewer than 1,000 members on its official roll. "No East European communist movement had been as pathetically weak and unsuccessful before it came to power as the Romanian," one scholar has noted.[1] If not for the strength of the Soviet

Union and the wishes of its dictator, Joseph Stalin—and the relative weakness and indifference of the Western Allies—Romania's Communists might have remained a fringe party and its postwar history would have followed a very different course.

Following the anti-German coup of August 1944, King Michael appointed a coalition government dominated by the National Peasant and Liberal parties. It included as minister of justice Lucretiu Patrascanu, who became the first Communist to hold a high-level post in Romanian government. Iuliu Maniu's National Peasants called for quick national elections, but were stymied by the Communists and their Soviet backers, who knew they stood no chance in a fair vote. Instead, the Communists agitated against the coalition government until it fell in late 1944.

Michael next named a pro-Western general, Nicolae Radescu, as premier. In a nod to the Communists, Radescu appointed one of their senior leaders, Teohari Georgescu, as undersecretary of the interior ministry, from which position he was able to insert fellow party members into key posts in the police and security forces. Meanwhile, the Communists stepped up their campaign to seize power completely, vilifying Radescu, shutting down newspapers, and using squads of goons to assault political opponents in the streets and stir up trouble.

In late February 1945, with chaos in the streets and Soviet tanks ringing the palace, Moscow issued an ultimatum to the king: Replace Radescu with Petru Groza, leader of the pro-Communist Plowmen's Front, or risk the possibility of an outright Soviet takeover. As an added inducement, the Russians promised that Romania would regain permanent control of Transylvania. With the West showing no support, Michael had little choice but to consent.

Groza became premier on March 6, 1945, a date that in many ways marks the real Communist seizure of power in Romania. Although it was nominally a coalition government—with discredited, dissident members of the National Peasant and Liberal parties in the cabinet—it was in fact a Communist regime in all but name. Groza appointed Communists to head the army as well as the interior, economic affairs, justice, and propaganda ministries. As one Communist leader put it, the new regime had the effect of "detaching Romania from the imperialist camp."[2] At Soviet urging, the government tried and executed Marshal Ion Antonescu and other senior members of his regime as war criminals in May and June.

Romania's postwar fate as a Soviet satellite had been secretly set at an October 1944 meeting in Moscow between Stalin and Prime Minister Winston Churchill of Great Britain. Churchill informally agreed that the Soviet Union could exercise 90 percent control in Romania in exchange for Britain being granted a similar free rein in Greece. Subsequent international conferences with the two leaders and President Franklin D. Roosevelt of the United States at Yalta in February 1945 and at Potsdam in the summer of that year did not recognize the prior agreement, but Stalin was to use it as justification for all subsequent Soviet actions in Romania.

The "Elections" of 1946 and 1948

The Romanian Communist Party (RCP) conducted an intense recruitment drive to build up its paltry numbers. From a mere 1,000 at war's end, the party swelled to more than 800,000 members by 1948 as many Romanians, clearly seeing which way the political wind was blowing, flocked to its banner. These new members included opportunists of all stripes, such as many ex-legionnaires of the fascist Iron Guard, whose politics theoretically were at the opposite end of the political spectrum from communism.

Meanwhile, the Communist leadership remained split between two main factions: the "home" Communists and the "Muscovites." The home Communists were native Romanians who mostly rose out of the labor movement and who had continued to operate underground in Romania during the war. Their leader was Gheorghe Gheorghiu-Dej, who had served a 12-year prison sentence after orchestrating a railroad strike in 1933. The Muscovites were Soviet-trained intellectuals, mostly nonethnic Romanians, who sat out the war in Moscow and returned to Bucharest with the Red Army. Their top leaders were Ana Pauker, a Moldavian Jew, and Vasile Luca, a Szekler from Transylvania who became a Soviet army major.

The two rival groups agreed to wary, joint leadership at the Communist Party's first annual conference in October 1945. Stalin naturally favored the Muscovites, who controlled most of the actual levers of power, but he consented to Gheorghiu-Dej's appointment as general secretary. The Soviets realized the need to grant the home Communists a role because most Romanians did not trust the Muscovites, regarding them as foreign interlopers in thrall to Stalin. (In particular, their backing for returning Bessarabia to the Soviet Union struck most Romanian nationalists as treachery.)

After months of Communist strong-arm tactics against the political opposition, Romanians voted in the promised national elections in November 1946. In balloting widely seen as fraudulent, the Communists and their leftist party allies claimed 90 percent of the vote and 379 of the 414 seats in the National Assembly. The Western Allies went on in February 1947 to sign a final peace treaty with Romania that formally recognized the country's current boundaries. The treaty also obliged Romania to respect political freedoms and human rights, commitments that the Groza regime promptly ignored.

The Cold War began in earnest in 1947 as the U.S.-led Western nations came to view Soviet actions in Eastern Europe as an aggressive threat to world peace. Stalin responded to the increased international tensions by ordering the Communists in the satellite states to seize complete power and toe Moscow's line on all matters. The obedient Romanian Communist Party launched a reign of terror against all its real and perceived political opponents, executing thousands and banishing the remainder to prison and work camps. National Peasant Party leader Iuliu Maniu, the most respected Romanian politician of his time, was given a life sentence on trumped-up charges of treason. He died in prison some years later.

In December 1947, Groza and Gheorghiu-Dej ordered King Michael to abdicate and leave the country or face civil war. He resisted as long as he could, but finally relented and went into exile in Switzerland. On December 30, the People's Republic of Romania was proclaimed.

Speaking of the docile Romanian people, Gheorghiu-Dej is reported to have cynically remarked: "Yesterday they were told to love the king, and they loved him. Today they are told to love us, and they will."[3]

Love, hate, or indifference—Romanians were given no real choice in the matter. The Communists joined with one wing of the Social Democratic Party to form the Romanian Workers' Party and, in March 1948, held the last elections that included the pretense of an opposition. The Communist-led Popular Democratic Front won 405 of the 414 seats.

In April, the National Assembly adopted a new constitution. Although on paper the assembly was the supreme structure of the state, in reality, the Communists, unmentioned in the document, ruled the country as a supragovernmental entity through the Politburo and the Council of Ministers. The constitution contained the usual meaningless provisions of political and civil rights and even "guaranteed" the right to own private property—except where the "general interest" dictated otherwise. That

Communist leader Gheorghe Gheorghiu-Dej, left, and Stefan Voitech, vice-president of the council of ministers, at a 1960 meeting of the U.N. General Assembly. (AP/Wide World Photos)

handy clause was invoked to nationalize the country's entire financial, banking, insurance, transportation, industrial, and mining enterprises in the months and years that followed.

The Department of State Security, known as the Securitate, was established and began its long history of surveillance and repression of all facets of Romanian society. The Orthodox Church came under government control, other religions were persecuted, Western influence was suppressed in favor of Slavic culture, Russian-language instruction was made mandatory, and the national history was rewritten to stress the Soviet Union's "glorious" role in Romania's "liberation."

On the economic front, the regime followed the pattern of other Soviet satellite states of Eastern Europe. Romania's agricultural system was forcibly collectivized from 1948 to 1962, as peasants were pushed to give up their private plots and work on large state-owned farms. Some 80,000 peasants who resisted the process were arrested as "class enemies." The program resulted in food shortages and drove many farmers out of rural areas in search of jobs in urban centers. Meanwhile, in common with other Stalinist economies, the regime's Five-Year Plans put most of its resources into developing heavy industry, such as steel-making, petrochemicals, and vast construction projects like the Danube-Black Sea Canal.

The Gheorghiu-Dej Years

It is widely agreed among historians and independent experts that the Soviet Union exploited Romania—"plundered" might be a better word—more thoroughly and ruthlessly than any other Eastern European nation, with the possible exception of East Germany. In the immediate aftermath of the war, the Soviets looted the Romanian economy of as much as $2 billion in factory equipment, shipping, railroad stock, and manufactured goods, carting it all back to Russia. In the years that followed, the Soviets also required Romania to continue paying stiff war reparations and to help defray the costs of the presence of Soviet troops in the country.

The Soviets ran Romania like a profit-making machine, for that is what it represented to them. Romania received only a small fraction of the investment loans and credits that Moscow granted to its other satellite nations. In 1949, Romania joined the Council for Mutual Economic Assistance (CMEA), more commonly known as Comecon. It was set up by the Soviet Union to foster economic cooperation and integration among its East European allies, mostly to Moscow's benefit. Like Germany before, the Soviet Union and the other more highly industrialized Comecon members saw Romania as a specialized source of food products and raw materials for the rest of the Eastern bloc, and so the Romanians were actively discouraged from developing their own heavy industry at the expense of agriculture.

Although Gheorghiu-Dej was himself a Stalinist at heart, he was a Stalinist for Romania, not Russia. He wanted to use the state's unchecked power to develop Romania's economy for its own people. In the parlance of the times, he was a "national Communist." But he had to keep his intentions under wraps because in the years after the 1948 Yugoslav-Soviet split (when Yugoslav leader Josip Broz Tito successfully broke away from Moscow's orbit) there were Stalin-inspired purges throughout the other satellite states of anyone who followed Tito's nationalist approach.

Stalin died in 1953. When Stalin's successor, Nikita Khrushchev, denounced him in 1956, Gheorghiu-Dej (although himself an ardent Stalinist) used Romania's ousted Muscovite faction as scapegoats for the earlier "excesses" of Romanian Communist rule. (Gheorghiu-Dej had purged the faction from the government in 1952.) Romania joined the Soviet-led Warsaw Pact military alliance in 1955, and backed the 1956 Soviet invasion that crushed Hungary's popular anticommunist revolution. But at the same time, Gheorghiu-Dej moved Romania onto an independent international course, pledging cooperation with any state, whether Communist or capitalist, so long as it respected Romania's sovereignty and did not meddle in its internal affairs. This stance led Romania to closer ties with Communist China, ruled by Mao Zedong, which advocated a similar course.

With Chinese backing, Gheorghiu-Dej craftily convinced Khrushchev to remove Soviet troops from Romania in 1957. Then, as the Sino-Soviet split came into the open in the late 1950s and early '60s, Romania was emboldened to increase its defiance of Moscow's dictates. While not throwing itself completely into the Chinese camp (as Albania did), Romania trod a delicate middle ground in the conflict. As one scholar subsequently noted: "On the overt basic issues of the Sino-Soviet dispute, [Gheorghiu-Dej] was always pro-Soviet; there was virtually no danger of his ever becoming a Maoist. Mao, to him, became simply a means of winning concessions from the Soviet Union."[4]

Under Gheorghiu-Dej's leadership, Romania took a number of increasingly bold steps: It forged ties with Tito's Yugoslavia, began soliciting credits from Western nations to finance Romania's industrial development, rebuffed Khrushchev's demands that it "integrate" its economy with Comecon (i.e., stress agriculture over industry), and commenced a "de-Russification" of Romanian politics and culture. These moves proved popular with the nationalistic Romanian people and were in line with Gheorghiu-Dej's goal: to replace Soviet backing for his regime with genuine popular support. Up until that point, "Moscow had protected its vassals from popular anger; now the people (and the West) should protect the regime from the fury of the Kremlin."[5]

Romania's campaign climaxed with the issuing of a Central Committee declaration on April 26, 1964. This so-called "Declaration of Independence" defiantly announced to Moscow and the world Romania's intention to go its own way in its economic affairs and international relations. It criticized both sides in the Sino-Soviet dispute. And it declared the Romanian party's complete autonomy from Soviet control: "No one can decide what is and what is not correct for other countries and parties. There is not and cannot be a 'parent' party and a 'son' party, a 'superior' and a 'subordinate' party."[6]

The Soviets could do nothing; Romania's carefully crafted provocations fell short of providing justification for a military invasion. Romania's position was further strengthened by the abrupt ouster of Khrushchev in October 1964 and his replacement by a more cautious Soviet leadership.

Gheorghiu-Dej died on March 19, 1965, at the age of 64, having achieved many of the aims he set out for himself and his country. Although he had presided over a period of terrible repression and wrenching social and economic changes in the 1950s, by the end of his life he had gained considerable respect both abroad and at home as a Romanian patriot.

He was succeeded by a triumvirate: Nicolae Ceausescu as party leader, Ion Gheorghe Maurer as premier, and Chivu Stoica as state council president. But it was Ceausescu who would quickly emerge on top, a position he would not relinquish until he had taken his country down a long road to ruin that reached its end with his violent overthrow nearly a quarter-century later.

Nicolae Ceausescu in a photo released in 1965, when he assumed the top post in the Romanian Communist Party. (AP/Wide World Photos)

The future dictator was only 47 when he was named first secretary of the Romanian Workers Party, but he had already been a Central Committee member for 13 years and a full Politburo member for 10. He had risen rapidly through the ranks due to his unswerving loyalty to Gheorghiu-Dej, whom he had met in prison during the war. He got along well with the working-class Gheorghiu-Dej: "The young Romanian peasant from the impoverished Olt valley who had become a Communist while still a teenager made a perfect acolyte; he was quick and shrewd, and had no tiresome pretensions to being an intellectual."[7]

Ceausescu's Consolidation of Power

Yet another Romanian constitution was adopted in 1965, after Gheorghiu-Dej's death. This nationalist document omitted all references to the Soviet Union and proclaimed that Romania was now a full-fledged "Socialist Republic" rather than merely a People's Republic, meaning the country had reached the final stage of development in Communist dogma. Underlining this supposed achievement, the Romanian Workers Party reverted to its previous name, the Romanian Communist Party.

The new leadership moved to demythologize Gheorghiu-Dej, criticizing his Stalinist policies and eradicating the "cult of personality" (emphasis on his personal greatness) that had been erected around him. There was little suspicion among his comrades that Ceausescu himself would soon build a similar cult around his own person that would make Gheorghiu-Dej seem positively modest by comparison.

Some of the Communist old guard probably hoped that they could control Ceausescu and keep him from gaining too much personal power. If so, they were to be sorely disappointed. He gradually eliminated all his major rivals and gained control of various key posts, including supreme military commander and state council president, while installing loyal followers in positions beneath him. By the time the Communist Party held its 10th party conference in 1969, Ceausescu exercised nearly absolute control over his regime.

In the initial years of his reign, Ceausescu traveled tirelessly around the country giving speeches to the masses, portraying himself as a Romanian nationalist and man of the people. The long-suffering population was given hope by his promises of loosened social controls, the rehabilitation of the reputations of some of Gheorghiu-Dej's political victims, and vows that the dreaded Securitate secret police would have to obey the rule of law.

Hopes were raised further as Ceausescu pushed his predecessor's independent foreign policy to new heights. In 1967 Romania established diplomatic relations with West Germany and then maintained ties with Israel after the rest of the Eastern bloc broke their ties in the wake of Israel's victory over the Arabs in the Six Day War. The crowning moment

Ceausescu's Early Years

The thick fog of mythology built up around Ceausescu's early life by later Communist historians has begun to lift in recent years, creating a more accurate picture. He was born on January 26, 1918, in the Walachian village of Scornicesti, the third son of a small-time farmer. He moved to Bucharest as a teenager—in part to escape his drunken, violent father—and briefly became an apprentice to his uncle, a shoemaker. He developed a reputation as a hooligan and was arrested for street brawling before joining the Young Communists' League. "Nicolae got involved for the violence rather than for the ideology," according to one well-placed Romanian historian.[8]

Certain exploits credited to him in his authorized biographies (such as his election to Romania's national anti-Fascist committee at the age of 15) were in fact attributable to his older brother Marin, who was subsequently kept out of the limelight to avoid embarrassing questions. A youthful contemporary of Nicolae recalls him as someone "whom everyone despised . . . He was dull, physically unprepossessing, on the small side, and afflicted with a risible stammer, which was so bad people avoided him—they didn't want to laugh in his face," especially because he was prone to unpredictable rages.[9]

Later, with the help of his wife Elena, whom he married in 1946 and who came to exercise great power over her husband, he conquered his stammer and became a passable public speaker. Both were poorly educated and harbored a lifelong distrust of intellectuals, although in their later years they were fulsomely celebrated as great thinkers and numerous books were ghost-written for them. In the view of a leading Romanian Communist, Silviu Brucan, Nicolae was "shrewd and smart," while Elena was "shrewd but stupid."[10] Such words, of course, were uttered only after their deaths.

came in 1968, when the forces of the Soviet-led Warsaw Pact invaded Czechoslovakia to crush the "Prague Spring" reformist government of Alexander Dubcek. Ceausescu openly condemned Moscow's aggression and refused the request for Romanian troops to join in the intervention.

For standing up to the Soviets, Ceausescu won praise not only from the West—French President Charles de Gaulle visited Romania in 1968 and U.S. President Richard Nixon followed suit in 1969—but from the

Romanian people as well. Intellectuals and artists flocked to join the Communist Party, believing that Ceausescu was allowing his own version of a reformist "Bucharest Spring" to develop. They did not see the danger that a homegrown totalitarianism was on the horizon that would be just as bad as the Soviet variety. "We have been so preoccupied with the danger of Soviet occupation that for all practical purposes we have pre-occupied ourselves," one Romanian prophetically observed at the time.[11]

Whatever his flaws, Ceausescu was perceived as first and foremost a nationalist. The writer Paul Goma, one of the few dissidents who stood up to the regime in its later phase, noted that during those early years,

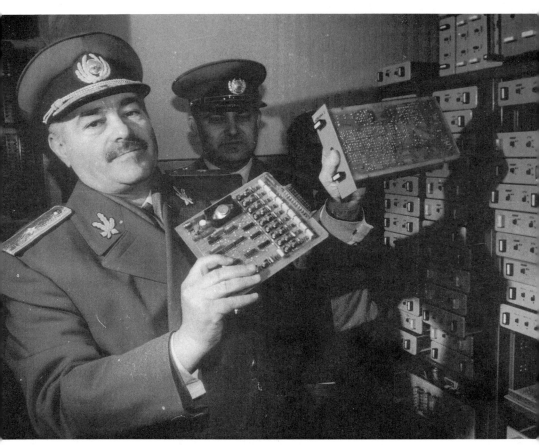

Wiretap gear of the dreaded Securitate secret police, who spied on all sectors of Romanian society. (AP/Wide World Photos)

"The general feeling was, among the vast majority of Romanians, Okay, he's a communist but at least he's against the Russians, the Hungarians, the Jews; he's one of *us*."[12]

But the members of the intelligentsia that joined the party ultimately found it to be a trap. "It was easy to join the Party [but] almost impossible to leave it because that meant abandoning both social life and one's profession," a Bucharest literature professor has said. "An intellectual who left the Party had two choices, to emigrate, or to become marginalized."[13]

So Ceausescu's promise of a political, social, and cultural opening in the late 1960s proved to be ephemeral. For careful observers, the writing was already on the wall as early as 1966, when Ceausescu first began implementing policies—such as restrictions on abortion, contraceptives, divorce, and emigration—that the West did not begin complaining about until the 1980s.

These policies grew in part out of Nicolae and Elena Ceausescu's strong puritanical streak: They opposed sexuality, drinking, smoking, and frivolity in general. They launched campaigns against "decadent" Western practices of the 1960s, such as long hair, beards, and miniskirts, and rejected the West's concepts of political and artistic freedom. "The common denominator of our socialist art is the Marxist-Leninist ideal," Ceausescu announced in 1968. In that same year he also proclaimed, "We do not understand democracy in its bourgeois meaning—of babbling, lack of discipline, anarchy. We understand democracy as the active participation of the citizens in formulating and implementing the Party's policy."[14]

Similarly, rather than reining in the Securitate as he had pledged, he allowed the secret police to flourish like some poisonous, choking weed. "It has been said that a good political machine thrives on the visibility of its rewards and the certainty of its punishments," one historian has noted. "Ceausescu's punishments were not ultimate—he killed only a few of his opponents—but they were certain: harassment, demotion, transfer, house arrest and prison. The Securitate penetrated deeply into the fabric of Romanian society, creating a pervasive atmosphere of fear by continually testing the loyalty of every citizen in the country and intimidating all but the most foolhardy."[15]

By the 1970s it had become clear that Ceausescu, a creative maverick in foreign affairs, was simply a small-minded tyrant at home. As one scholar put it in 1988, before the collapse of communism:

In foreign policy the communists inherited and continued the best and most skillful characteristics of the old regime; in domestic policy they took over some of the worst and amplified them. Nationalist and resourceful in foreign policy, the Bucharest regime under Ceausescu became tyrannical and unresourceful at home, with all those characteristics of nepotism, corruption, and indifference to popular needs that had disfigured Romania's prewar governmental systems. Romania came to be considered the worst-governed East European country . . . What steadily developed in Romania during the 1970s can loosely be described as neo-Stalinism without terror. The result was creeping disintegration.[16]

"Pharaonic" Socialism

A turning point in Ceausescu's rule came when he and Elena visited the Far East in 1971, where they were deeply influenced by what they saw in Communist China and North Korea. In China under Mao Zedong, the Cultural Revolution—a violent, anti-intellectual purge aimed at eradicating all vestiges of capitalism and Western influence—was in full swing. Elena was apparently particularly impressed by the prominence and power being wielded by Mao's wife, Jiang Qing. The Ceausescus were also fascinated by North Korean dictator Kim Il Sung and his penchant for glorifying his rule with massive building projects. They were enamored with his super-orderly capital, Pyongyang, with its wide, empty avenues and endless rows of identical apartment blocks.

The Ceausescus would eventually transplant these modern versions of Oriental despotism back to their homeland, creating a monstrous cult of personality around themselves, "the sheer ludicrousness of which insulted, humiliated, angered or amused most Romanians."[17] Thus commenced the period of what some observers have called "pharaonic socialism" (a reference to the pharaohs, the all-powerful god-kings of ancient Egypt who had the pyramids built as eternal monuments to their greatness). The process began when, on his return from Asia, Ceausescu promulgated his "July theses," which called for a stringent discipline in cultural affairs.

The pharaonic phase, which grew steadily worse until the revolution of 1989, has also been characterized as "dynastic socialism," or rule by a family dynasty rather than the Communist Party. Increasingly suspicious, even paranoid, of his enemies, Ceausescu in the late 1970s and early 1980s promoted unqualified but loyal family members—his wife, his son Nicu (who had a well-justified reputation as a "socialist playboy"), three of his brothers, and a brother-in-law—to influential posts in the ministries of science and technology, party cadres, youth, defense, and internal affairs.

Aside from family members, Ceausescu surrounded himself with sycophants who agreed to everything he proposed, no matter how outrageous—a form of government that one scholar dubbed a "sycophan-tocracy." Elena became the most powerful woman in the Eastern bloc, joining the Politburo in 1973 and ultimately becoming first deputy premier. Despite her limited educational background, she claimed to be a world-

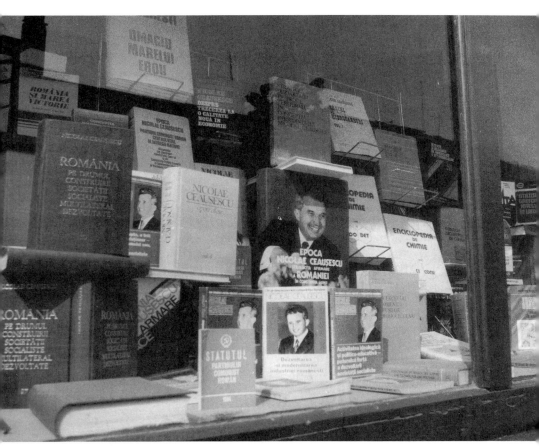

Volumes "written" by and about Ceausescu dominate a Bucharest bookstore's window display in 1988. (AP/Wide World Photos)

class chemist and engineer, and was celebrated as an "eminent personage of Romanian and international science."

Still more fulsome praise was heaped on her husband. His dictatorship was referred to as the "Epoch of Light" and the "Golden Age." The list of his attributes was endless: He was "the Genius of the Carpathians," the "savior of the nation," the "hero of peace," the "most brilliant revolutionary thinker of all times," the "torchbearer among torchbearers," "unique as a mountain peak," and, despite his stammering, "our famous lullaby trill"—all of these qualities tempered by his "saintly modesty." Ceausescu apparently came to believe that the huge crowds organized by party functionaries to applaud him wherever he went were genuine evidence of his popular adoration, when they were in fact "a permanent ceremonial enacted by the entire country in front of a single spectator."[18]

Although they could not say so in public, most Romanians undoubtedly found this personality cult ridiculous. Nevertheless, if the eccentricities of Ceausescu's rule had been restricted to phony accolades and grandiose monuments, his fellow countrymen could probably have learned to live with them. Much more damaging, however, were the drastic economic and social policies that he was able to implement due to his unchecked power. These could not be laughed off.

Following his primitive Stalinist instincts, Ceausescu sought to underline Romania's national independence by pouring virtually all of the country's resources into heavy industry at the expense of agriculture, building high-risk, uneconomical steel mills, petrochemical plants, and shipyards, and restarting work on the monumental (and unnecessary) Danube-Black Sea canal. At first Romania was able to afford these projects thanks to an influx of loans from Western nations, especially after 1972 when it became the first Comecon country to join the International Monetary Fund (IMF) and World Bank.

For the first half of the 1970s, Romania actually seemed to be enjoying a period of prosperity, although it was a hollow one that could not last. As its own petroleum resources dwindled, it turned to importing oil from the Middle East, forging close relations with the Arab states and Iran. But as the price of oil skyrocketed in the mid-1970s, Romania's foreign debt rose accordingly, and by 1980 it owed $11 billion to the West. In 1981 Romania was on the verge of bankruptcy and became the second Comecon country (Poland was the first) to have to reschedule its debt payments to Western bankers.

In the early 1980s, in a typically idiosyncratic move that verged on economic lunacy, Ceausescu launched a crash program to pay off all of Romania's foreign debts within a decade, declaring that interest payments to the West were equivalent to the tribute Romanians had previously paid to the Ottoman Empire. The regime cut domestic electricity usage, slashed imports and stepped up exports, particularly from the agricultural sector.

As a result, life for the vast majority of Romanians—never luxurious even in the best of times—became one of unrelieved misery. People were restricted to one 40 watt lightbulb per room, central heating plants kept wintertime temperatures in apartment complexes in the low 50s Fahrenheit (that is, when heat was available, sometimes only for a few hours a day), and hot water was frequently unavailable for weeks at a time.

Despite rationing, food was hard to come by for most people, as most of the country's agricultural wealth was being exported for hard currency. Showing how out of touch with reality he really was, Ceausescu in 1982 accused his countrymen of being too fat and launched an effort to reduce Romanians' caloric intake through a "program of scientific nourishment." The Ceausescus themselves sought to practice what they preached. They were "weight-watchers and food freaks. They were natural converts to organic food, as much on their guard against poisoning by impurities as by their enemies . . . When Ceausescu said Romanians would do better to eat less it was not just the remark of a cynical dictator. He was offering a piece of royal wisdom. The ruling pair set an example by their own leanness."[19]

While Romania became the "Ethiopia of Europe," the regime lied to itself and the world. In late 1989, shortly before he was overthrown, Ceausescu announced a bumper grain harvest of 60 million tons, when the actual total was less than 17 million tons.

The Romanian people themselves were not deceived, but there was not much they could do about it. There were widespread protests by factory workers in 1987, but the demonstrations were quickly crushed with hundreds of arrests. (The regime had reacted similarly after one of the few earlier outbreaks of unrest, a strike by miners in the Jiu Valley region in 1977.)

As one observer has put it:

> Ceausescu had done what none of his Soviet-bloc colleagues dared:
> break the unwritten contract between Communists and the working

class. Fearful of the consequences of admitting economic failure and the need for sacrifices, the other leaders had gone on borrowing in the West largely to keep living standards artificially high . . . Ceausescu had the nerve to do what the other East European leaders were often tempted to but never dared: treat his working class as harshly as he thought they deserved.[20]

As if the daily grind of huddling in cold, dark rooms and scavenging for food was not bad enough, Ceausescu increased the misery index still further with various cruel social policies. One of the most notorious was his "pro-birth" program, a misguided effort to increase Romania's population by banning abortions and the sale of contraceptives. The policy was originally implemented in 1966 and was made still more intrusive in the 1980s when the regime actually began requiring monthly gynecological checkups of women at their workplaces to ensure that if a woman became pregnant she would be forced to carry her pregnancy to term.

This bizarre experiment in Orwellian Big Brotherhood backfired horribly. Far from permanently increasing the birth rate, by the mid-1980s the rate was back to where it had been in 1966. Its main effect was a huge increase in the death rate among pregnant women, which jumped from 86 deaths per 100,000 live births in 1966 to 150 in 1984, with most of the increase attributable to botched, illegal abortions. Many of the women who did give birth were too poor to care for their babies and were forced to abandon them. Thousands of infants (many of whom contracted the AIDS virus due to a widespread Romanian medical practice of unchecked blood transfusions) were warehoused in wretched state orphanages, a haunting legacy that will be explored in more detail in a later chapter.

The other, most glaring example of Ceausescu's social engineering was his policy of "systemization" and "modernization" of the Romanian countryside. This "rural urbanization" program aimed at demolishing thousands of Romania's ancient and historic towns and villages—those considered "irrational" and "nonviable"—and moving their inhabitants against their will into poorly constructed suburban housing projects ("agro-industrial centers") where they would supposedly have greater access to government services.

The systemization strategy, originally developed in the 1970s, was further elaborated by Ceausescu in the late 1980s. Fortunately for most Romanians, the cash-strapped regime did not have the resources to carry

"The house that Ceausescu built": The grandiose People's Palace, supposedly the second-largest building in the world, was opened to the public after the revolution. (AP/Wide World Photos)

out the program on a large scale. Nevertheless, thousands of Romanians were forced to evacuate their homes and watch them get bulldozed, and many village churches were razed. The program also caused a major crisis in Romania's relations with Hungary in 1988. Many ethnic Hungarian villages in Transylvania were targeted for destruction, the latest step in Romania's longstanding effort to forcibly assimilate its Hungarian minority.

By this stage, Romania had succeeded in alienating itself from both the East and the West. Ceausescu strongly resisted Soviet leader Mikhail Gorbachev's calls for reform, and the Bucharest regime came to be considered an embarrassment to the other more moderate East European Communist states. Meanwhile Western nations, after years of smiling upon Ceausescu because of his independence from Moscow, finally grew weary of his unpredictable behavior and appalling human rights record. The United States was on the verge of revoking Romania's most favored nation (MFN) trading status in 1988 when Ceausescu himself preemptively renounced it.

There is one more aspect of Ceausescu's misrule that deserves comment: He did not spare the Romanian capital from the destruction his policies had wrought in the countryside. Ever since returning from North Korea in 1971, he had longed to reproduce Pyongyang's sterile, monumental architecture in Bucharest. Damage from an earthquake in 1977 gave him the excuse to order the demolition to begin. Elaborate plans were laid, and in 1984 an entire city district housing 40,000 people—and including beautiful, historic architecture, churches, and a monastery—was leveled to clear the way for the Victory of Socialism Boulevard and a massive complex of government buildings.

The only structure that was nearly completed when Ceausescu was ousted was the 6,000-room People's Palace, also known as the House of the Republic. It was meant to be the largest building in the world, although the Pentagon, which houses the U.S. Department of Defense in Washington, D.C., apparently still owns that honor. At a cost of untold millions of dollars, 17,000 men worked 24 hours a day on the project, guarded by Securitate agents and constantly supervised by Ceausescu ("Dracula driving a bulldozer"[21]) and his wife. Today the People's Palace stands empty, a fitting epitaph to the "Epoch of Light."

Virtually all observers agree that, even if it is not the largest building in the world, it is certainly one of the ugliest. "Here, the Communist-pharaonic disease of gigantism reached its apogee"[22] in a "monument to vandalism as well as megalomania."[23]

Western students of Romanian history have had some difficulty coming to grips with Ceausescuism. Romanian-born scholar Nestor Ratesh perhaps put it best when he wrote:

> Some intellectual endeavor was devoted to finding a formula that described the peculiarity of the Ceausescu regime in the 1970s and 1980s. For some, it was a primitive Stalinism. Others added a touch of Byzantine tradition to the classical communist totalitarianism, and still others spoke of an ersatz society, a pseudo-neo-Stalinism. There might have been a bit of all these ingredients, although in the end it looked in many respects like pure madness.[24]

NOTES

1. J. F. Brown, *Eastern Europe and Communist Rule*, p. 267.
2. Edward Behr, *Kiss the Hand You Cannot Bite*, p. 108.
3. Ibid.
4. J. F. Brown, *The New Eastern Europe: The Khrushchev Era and After*, p. 206.
5. Paul Lendvai, *Eagles in Cobwebs*, p. 301.
6. Ibid, p. 309.
7. Mark Frankland, *The Patriots' Revolution*, p. 299.
8. Behr, op. cit., p. 56.
9. Ibid, p. 57.
10. Frankland, op. cit., p. 312.
11. Michael Shafir, *Romania—Politics, Economics and Society*, p. 150.
12. Behr, op. cit., p. 146.
13. Frankland, op. cit., p. 99.
14. Behr, op. cit., p. 147.
15. Gale Stokes, *The Walls Came Tumbling Down*, p. 57.
16. J. F. Brown, *Eastern Europe and Communist Rule*, p. 275.
17. Ibid, p. 276.
18. Stokes, op. cit., p. 54.
19. Frankland, op. cit., p. 297.
20. Ibid, p. 306.
21. Behr, op. cit., p. 219.
22. Eva Hoffman, *Exit into History: A Journey Through the New Eastern Europe*, p. 308.
23. J. F. Brown, *Eastern Europe and Communist Rule*, p. 282.
24. Nestor Ratesh, *Romania: The Entangled Revolution*, p. 3.

5

Revolution

In 1989, with Communist regimes around Eastern Europe toppling like a row of dominoes, Romania stood alone. But even there, some of the first signs of overt dissent had begun to appear. Literature professor Doina Cornea and poets Mircea Dinescu and Anna Blandiana raised their voices in daring public protests. Three editors from *Romania Libera* (Free Romania), the country's second-largest official newspaper, were arrested when they attempted to publish an anti-Ceausescu edition. (They were sentenced to death but were spared by the revolution.) Even the government's official representative to the United Nations Commission on Human Rights was placed under house arrest after he issued a report highly critical of the regime's abuses.

But the most significant development came in the spring of 1989 when a group of six leading Romanian Communists and former senior government officials sent Ceausescu an open letter harshly criticizing his dictatorial rule. This famous "Letter of Six" was drafted by Marxist theoretician Silviu Brucan and signed by him and five others, including former foreign minister Corneliu Manescu, former party first secretary Gheorghe Apostol, and party founding member Constantin Pirvulescu, then 94 years old. The letter accused Ceausescu of suspending the constitution, violating the 1975 Helsinki Accords on human rights (which Romania had signed), destroying Bucharest in the name of rebuilding it, wrecking the economy and agriculture, and indulging in "harebrained schemes" to modernize the country.

Ceausescu ignored the letter and had its signers placed under house arrest or banished to internal exile. Nevertheless, it was widely publicized abroad and alerted Romanians to the fact that even veteran elements of the Communist establishment had lost all faith in their leader. The country seemed to hold its collective breath, waiting for something to happen, assuming someone else would start it, whatever *it* was. "It was like waiting for a train," a leading intellectual said. "You knew it would come, but you didn't know when."[1]

As if nothing were amiss, the Romanian Communist Party went ahead with its 14th Party Conference in late November. Unanimously "reelected" president, Ceausescu gave his usual six-hour speech, interrupted by "stormy applause," in which he criticized Romania's neighbors for not behaving like good socialists.

Plotters may indeed have been waiting in the wings, but a spark was needed to ignite the flimsy tinderbox that Ceausescu's regime had become. That spark would flare in a most unlikely place.

The Timisoara Trigger

The place was Timisoara, a charming city in western Romania. Although some regard it as being in Transylvania, it is more accurately described as the capital of the Banat region, where for centuries Hungarians, Saxons, Serbians, and other, smaller ethnic minorities had lived peaceably alongside the Romanian majority. This ethnic harmony, unusual for Romania, was in fact a crucial element that helps explain the solidarity that Timisoara displayed in rising up against Ceausescu in December 1989.

Since most Romanians regard Hungarians with suspicion, it is ironic that the trigger for the rebellion was a Hungarian Protestant pastor, Rev. Laszlo Tokes of the Reformed Church. He had become an irritant to the regime, publicly criticizing its abuses, especially the "systemization" program to destroy rural villages. Earlier in the year, he had been ordered to transfer from Timisoara to a remote village parish. When he refused to go, an embarrassed church hierarchy asked the government to evict him from his church.

On December 15, the deadline for eviction, a thousand people gathered in the square outside the church. Initially, they were mostly Hungarians, but they were quickly joined by Romanians, Serbs, and others. Clashes with police and militia broke out, but the deadline passed with Tokes unevicted. The next day the crowds swelled to as many as 10,000, joined by students and other young people, and the protests took on the character of a full-fledged anticommunist uprising. Shouts of "Down with Ceausescu," "Down with the dictator," and "Today in Timisoara, tomorrow in the whole country" rang out in the streets. Troops were mobilized to stop the marchers, although there was no gunfire and there were no deaths (apparently most of the soldiers had been issued unloaded weapons). Late on the night of December 16, Securitate agents stormed the church and beat and arrested Tokes. But it was too late, for he had already served his purpose—the revolution had begun.

An enraged Ceausescu, joined by his wife, Elena, called an emergency meeting of the party's Political Executive Committee December 17 in Bucharest. (The meeting was tape-recorded and a transcript was later released.) He ranted that the Timisoara uprising was a foreign plot, hatched in Washington and Moscow and carried out by Hungarian agents. He lambasted Defense Minister Gen. Vasile Milea, Interior Minister Tudor Postelnicu, and the Securitate chief, Gen. Iulian Vlad, for not arming the anti-riot troops with live ammunition to suppress the "hooligans."

"They should have fired to bring them down, to warn them, and then to fire at their legs . . . You don't put an enemy down with sermons, you have to burn him," Ceausescu shouted. Elena pitched in: "You should have fired on them, and had they fallen, you should have taken them and shoved them into a cellar. Weren't you told that? Not one of them should have gotten out."[2]

The committee then approved Ceausescu's formal order to arm the troops in Timisoara and "wherever there is an attempt of [antigovernment] action, liquidate it radically, without a word."[3] After the dictator made a false threat to resign, his aides fell to their knees and promised to carry out his orders. Mollified, and demonstrating a surreal sense of confidence totally unjustified by the circumstances, Ceausescu left early the next morning for a long-planned three-day state visit to Iran.

December 17 was "Bloody Sunday" in Timisoara. Milea and Vlad were not among the anti-Ceausescu plotters but they could see which way the wind was blowing and apparently had no intention of carrying out the dictator's bloodthirsty orders. Perhaps suspecting this, Ceausescu had already dispatched a key aide, Ion Coman, to Timisoara to take command and carry out the shoot-to-kill policy. That evening, uniformed soldiers and plainclothes agents opened fire on the huge crowd gathered in the central square. The shooting continued for the next two days.

The actual death toll remains in dispute to this day. Initial reports in the foreign news media suggested that many thousands had died. It is possible that this was a deliberate exaggeration by the anti-Ceausescu plotters in order to fan the flames of popular rebellion. The official count from the post-revolutionary government was around 100, and this may be closer to the truth. But whatever the total, it was clear that a major massacre had taken place. Romanians throughout the country heard about the bloodshed on shortwave radio from Radio Free Europe and other foreign broadcasts, prompting strikes and protests to break out in other cities.

By December 20 the tide had turned in Timisoara. Many rank-and-file soldiers were sickened by what they had been ordered to do and began fraternizing with the people, prompting the crowds to begin chanting: "The army is with us!" The anti-Ceausescu plotters had apparently gained sufficient control of the military command structure to prevent further futile efforts to crush the Timisoara uprising. The first revolutionary committees were formed, and Timisoara essentially became a "free city." The main theater of resistance now shifted to Bucharest.

The Flight and Death of the Ceausescus

Ceausescu returned from Iran on December 20 and began to grasp the seriousness of the situation. In a speech broadcast to the nation that night he again charged that the unrest in Timisoara was an "imperialist"

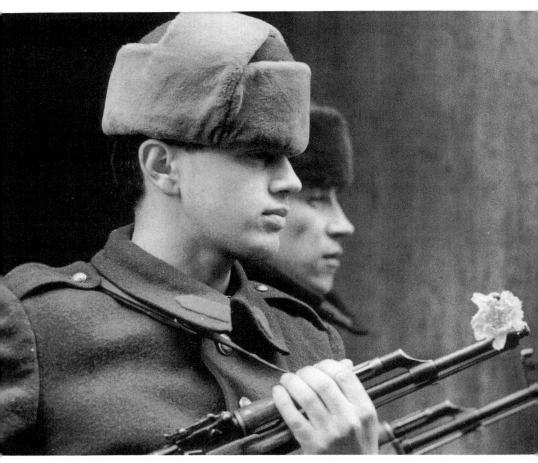

"The army is with us!" A Romanian soldier on guard after the military switched to the people's side in the revolution. (AP/Wide World Photos)

superpower plot designed to destroy socialism in Romania using "Fascist" Hungarian agents and hooligans. It was an unconvincing message.

The next day, December 21, Ceausescu made the last of the many mistakes he had made during his nearly 25 years in power, and it proved to be the fatal one. He decided to greet the people, "his" people, with a rousing speech from the balcony of the Central Committee building overlooking the Palace Square. He expected applause, and why not? "Is any dictator so entirely calculating and cynical that he can avoid falling victim to the system he creates, and himself remain undazzled by the flattery it so efficiently produces?"[4]

This time, the crowd of thousands was not stocked with tame Ceausescu loyalists—there were none left. Several minutes into the speech, the first shouts of "Timisoara!" and "Ceausescu, dictator!" could be heard on the live television broadcast. Ceausescu looked helplessly at his wife, who responded by saying, "Promise them something!" It was too late for that. The broadcast was interrupted, but before the screen went blank for good it was clear to viewers that the square had dissolved into chaos, and the entire nation could see that their vaunted emperor had no clothes.

After that epochal moment, the end came quickly. The following day, December 21, Bucharest radio announced that Defense Minister Milea had committed suicide after being exposed as a "traitor." Many observers believe he was executed by Ceausescu after he refused to order the army to fire on the people. Whatever the case, his death helped convince wavering senior officers to throw in their lot with the revolution.

Later that day Ceausescu made one more pathetic effort to address the crowd from his balcony, but the microphone did not work and a mob was already entering the building. Ceausescu, his wife, two top aides, and two bodyguards barely had time to climb to the roof and escape in a waiting helicopter. But their pilot betrayed them. Rather than taking them to a place of safety, he set them down on a road outside the capital. There they commandeered a car from a passing motorist but were eventually captured by soldiers and taken to an army base in the town of Tirgoviste. The base commander was ordered by the new provisional regime taking shape in Bucharest to hold them until it could send representatives to conduct a trial.

For periods over the next two days their captors kept the Ceausescus prisoner inside an armored vehicle that kept circling around the base as protection against any rescue attempt by Securitate loyalists. On December 25, a military tribunal was hastily organized and Nicolae and Elena Ceausescu were tried in a judicial proceeding that all observers subsequently agreed was little more than a "kangaroo court." The Ceausescus did not recognize the authority of the tribunal and treated their prosecutors with disdain, and they in turn heaped scorn upon the accused. The "defense counsel" provided to the couple did not dispute any of the charges and insisted that the proceeding was a "legal trial." He tried in vain to convince his clients to plead insanity.

The "Trial" of the Ceausescus

What follows are excerpts from a transcript of the closed military trial of Nicolae and Elena Ceausescu, held on December 25, 1989, and broadcast the following day on Romanian television.[5]

PROSECUTOR: Esteemed chairman of the court, today we have to pass a verdict on the defendants Nicolae Ceausescu and Elena Ceausescu who have committed the following offenses: Crimes against the people. They carried out acts that are incompatible with human dignity and social thinking, they acted in a despotic and criminal way, they destroyed the people whose leaders they claimed to be. Because of the crimes they committed against the people, I plead, on behalf of the victims of these two tyrants, for the death sentence for the two defendants . . .

CEAUSESCU: I will answer any question, but only at the Grand National Assembly, before the representatives of the working class. Tell the people that I will answer all their questions. All the world should know what is going on here. I only recognize the working class and the Grand National Assembly—no one else.

PROSECUTOR: The Grand National Assembly has been dissolved.

CEAUSESCU: This is not possible at all. No one can dissolve the National Assembly.

PROSECUTOR: We now have another leading organ. The National Salvation Front is now our supreme body.

CEAUSESCU: No one recognizes that. That is why the people are fighting all over the country. This gang will be destroyed. They organized the putsch.

PROSECUTOR: The people are fighting against you, not against the new forum . . .

CEAUSESCU: Nobody can change the state structures. This is not possible. Usurpers have been punished severely during the past cen-

In the videotape made of the closed hearing the prosecutors' faces are not shown. However, it seemed the protagonists knew each other. "Do you know who is holding you?" a tribunal member asked at one point. "Yes," Ceausescu replied. "Securitate." At another point, Elena said, "I was like a mother to you."[6]

turies in Romania's history. Nobody has the right to abolish the Grand National Assembly.

PROSECUTOR: Did you know about the genocide in Timisoara?

ELENA CEAUSESCU: What genocide? By the way, I will not answer any more questions.

PROSECUTOR: Did you know about the genocide or did you, as a chemist, deal only with polymers? You, as a scientist, did you know about it?

CEAUSESCU: Her scientific papers were published abroad!

PROSECUTOR: And who wrote the papers for you, Elena?

ELENA CEAUSESCU: Such impudence! I am a member and the chairwoman of the Academy of Sciences. You cannot talk to me in such a way! .

PROSECUTOR: You have never been able to hold a dialogue with the people . . . You held monologues and the people had to applaud, like in the rituals of tribal people. And today you are acting in the same megalomaniac way. Now we are making a last attempt. Do you want to sign this statement?

CEAUSESCU: No, we will not sign. And I also do not recognize the counsel for the defense . . .

DEFENSE COUNSEL: Please make a note that here it has been stated that all legal regulations have been observed, that this is a legal trial. Therefore, it is a mistake for the two accused to refuse to cooperate with us. This is a legal trial and I honor them by defending them . . . I ask the court, as the plaintiff, to take note that proof has been furnished for all these points, that the two have committed the offenses mentioned. . . .

PROSECUTOR: Esteemed Mr. Chairman, I have been one of those who, as a lawyer, would have liked to oppose the death sentence, because it is inhuman. But we are not talking about people. I would not call for the death sentence, but it would be incomprehensible for the Romanian people to have to go on suffering this great misery and not to have it ended by sentencing the two Ceausescus to death . . .

After a trial lasting several hours, the Ceausescus were found guilty of all charges: genocide, massacre, destruction of communal property, economic subversion, attempted escape, and the hoarding of more than $1 billion in Swiss bank accounts. The sentence was death, and it was carried out virtually within minutes of the end of the trial. As the reality of their situation finally set in on the doomed couple, Elena reportedly said, "Look, they're going to shoot us like dogs. I can't believe this. Is the death penalty still in force in Romania?"[7]

The execution was not filmed, supposedly because the eager squad of soldiers started shooting before the cameraman could get outside. The Ceausescus were lined up against a courtyard wall and riddled with bullets. According to one account, however, the soldiers were beaten to the punch by two members of the tribunal—Virgil Magureanu and Gelu Voican Voiculescu—who killed the couple with close-range pistol shots. Both men went on to influential posts in the new government, Magureanu as head of the new intelligence service.

A videotape of the Ceausescus' dead bodies, along with a short, edited version of the trial, was broadcast on Romanian television the next day, December 26. A longer three-hour tape of the proceedings was not released until months later. The farcical nature of the staged trial and the hasty executions struck a sour note in the minds of many Romanians and was criticized abroad. The new regime's excuse was that immediate proof of the dictator's death was necessary to convince loyalist Securitate elements who were still battling in the streets of Bucharest to give up the fight. But many people reached another conclusion, that Ceausescu had to be killed before he could disclose secrets that the men who were maneuvering to replace him did not want revealed.

Dissident writer Paul Goma stated that by ordering the mock trial and summary executions, the new regime "stole Ceausescu from those who suffered because of him" and "accomplished the extraordinary, the unheard and undeserved feat of turning the Ceausescus into human beings."[8]

The "Tele-Revolution"

The truth about the bloodshed and chaos in the city of Bucharest from December 22 to 25 remains elusive. There was fierce street fighting the likes of which had not been seen in Europe since World War II. Hundreds of people died, mostly civilians. A new, post-Ceausescu government rose up virtually overnight, proclaiming itself the voice of the people's revolution. But the question remains: Precisely who was shooting at whom, and to what purpose?

Certain surface facts are clear. The revolution was essentially over when the Ceausescus fled. The army, which up until that point had still been firing on demonstrators in the streets, switched its allegiance to the people—or, more specifically, to the National Salvation Front (NSF), which first proclaimed its existence in a December 22 broadcast to the nation.

Although the new ruling body included a smattering of dissident intellectuals who had taken a leading role in the uprising, the NSF consisted primarily of "former" Communist members of the Ceausescu regime as well as ex- and current officers of the military and Securitate. Their undisputed leader was Ion Iliescu, 60, a former Ceausescu protege who had fallen out of the dictator's good graces in the 1970s. The smoothness with which he moved into the top leadership spot reinforced speculation of the prior existence of a plot against Ceausescu. Indeed, it was later reported that some generals switched to the side of the revolution only on the condition that "serious politicians" take power rather than "a few crazy poets and intellectuals."[9]

However, it was just such "crazy" people—courageous would be a more accurate term—who presented the public, romantic face of the Romanian revolt that was seen by their fellow countrymen as well as by the world at large in the tumultuous days that followed. That is because Romania's was perhaps the world's first "tele-revolution." Journalists, writers, poets, and students took over Bucharest's television station and rallied the nation by broadcasting live reports of the fighting and breathless appeals to action as gunfire crackled outside the studio. As Andrei Codrescu put it, "The Revolution is Televised: Seize the Means of Projection!"[10]—a pun on the standard Communist rhetoric about seizing the means of production.

And it was young people, mostly students, who paid the price of blood in the streets, manning barricades alongside soldiers and being shot down by mysterious snipers. Their sacrifices prompted one Romanian to re-proach himself for believing that young people "had only disco, rock videos, and loud entertainment in their heads . . . What a bitter lesson in civics they taught us! What a history lesson, written in blood! How immature we so-called adults seem all of a sudden!"[11]

These poignant images were witnessed by a worldwide audience, as one Romanian-American commenator noted:

> Watching the Romanian revolution on CNN [Cable News Network],
> people all over the world were struck by just how *revolutionary* the
> Romanian revolution was. The scenes they were seeing were
> reminiscent of the French and Bolshevik revolutions, living tableaux.
> The people atop tanks with their arms stretched in the victory sign,
> banners behind them . . . The tricolor armbands, the headbands . . .
> a beautifully photogenic but nonetheless horribly bloody revolution,
> summoned, it seemed, from historical skies by France itself . . ."[12]

A new, heady feeling of freedom gripped the populace in the days and
weeks that followed, and common people were emboldened to speak
openly to foreigners for the first time in their lives.

> It was as if they were trying to throw off a lifetime of caution in a few
> moments. They told us their names, their addresses, their life stories,
> the stories of their families, their own versions of their country's
> history. They even recited lists of American presidents— proud of the
> hitherto forbidden knowledge . . . Foreign journalists in those first
> few days after the revolution had become priests, privy to the
> unconfessed secrets of everyone.[13]

Popular Uprising or Coup?

What was the source of the stubborn, murderous resistance against the
revolution that persisted from December 22 to 25, and that waned only
after the preemptive execution of the Ceausescus? Who were the army
and their civilian allies fighting against? Initially the resisters were labeled
Securitate, then criminals, and finally simply terrorists. Wild, unprovable
rumors circulated: The terrorists were special forces—much better armed,
trained, and equipped than the regular Romanian army—from
Ceausescu's personal guard who operated outside the regular Securitate
chain of command. They included a cadre of robot-like fanatics, taken as
children from orphanages and raised to be brainwashed super-soldiers
who would fight for their dictator with blind obedience, pumped full of
drugs to make them abnormally strong. They were supported by scores
of Palestinian, Libyan, and Iranian terrorists, foreign mercenaries brought
into the country by helicopter to rescue Ceausescu and wreak havoc.

The stories amounted to a mix of fact and paranoid fantasy. No solid evidence has emerged of the crazed "orphan brigade." But Ceausescu may have had secret military agreements with Libya and Iran (whether they were ever activated is another question), and there were a few Palestinian guerrillas undergoing training in Romania who apparently became involved in the fighting. And there is no question that the terrorists were well-trained killers armed with exotic weapons—like sniper rifles with night-vision scopes—who spread panic by traveling via a secret tunnel system beneath Bucharest and popping up out of manholes to shoot unsuspecting victims.

The bloodshed was real enough. Hundreds died in Bucharest, more than had been killed in Timisoara, although interestingly most of the dead were civilians, not soldiers. (The official death toll for the entire revolution was later put at more than 1,000.) But what first raised people's suspicions

This hospital morgue in Bucharest is stacked with victims of the "terrorist" phase of the street fighting. The Romanian flag overhead has had the Communist symbol cut out from its center. (AP/Wide World Photos)

was the fate of those terrorists—and there were quite a few—who were wounded, captured, or surrendered in the days after Ceausescu's execution. They all essentially disappeared from jails and hospital beds, and none were ever brought to public trial or made available for questioning. By August 1990, the new government said it was still investigating 1,456 people, of whom 30 had been convicted and 69 others were still being tried. But all these cases involved crimes committed before December 22, 1989; that is, they were unrelated to the "terrorist" phase of the Bucharest fighting.

Iliescu himself was elusive when questioned about the identity of the "terrorists" in 1990, after he became president. "It's the most obscure problem," he said. "History will clarify these things one way or the other. It is possible that some of them will forever remain a riddle . . . I myself cannot name even those who possess all these secrets."[14]

There were a host of other unresolved questions, some of which were obvious to anyone who examined the devastation in central Bucharest following the fighting. In Palace Square the only structure that escaped unscathed was the Central Committee building, in which the NSF leadership gathered during the crucial days and on the balcony of which they even appeared to exhort the population to resist. But nearby buildings of no obvious military significance—such as the Royal Palace, which housed the national art museum, and the university library—were virtually destroyed, at great cultural cost. Similarly, the television station survived with only a few bullet holes, while structures around it were heavily damaged or flattened. No attempt was made to blow up the TV antennae or cut power to the station.

Much of the damage was caused by indiscriminate tank fire by inexperienced soldiers. But many people wondered why the terrorists, presumably well-schooled in urban commando tactics, did not take the most obvious military steps to squelch the revolution: Attack the NSF leadership and silence the broadcast facilities that were rallying the nation. Other questions arose in the weeks and months that followed, such as why were high-ranking army and Securitate officers implicated in the Timisoara massacre promoted to high posts in the new government.

Romanians have a national tendency to see the hidden hand of conspiracy behind most public events, but in this case they seem to be well-justified in their suspicions. The problem is that there are too many conspiracy theories to choose from, and they cannot all be correct. One major theme of the critics is that the fighting in Bucharest following Ceausescu's fall was "an 'operetta war,' a staged affair in which only the victims were real," Nestor Ratesh wrote. "According to these critics, this mini-war was meant to legitimize the new power, to give it the aura and prestige of the savior of the revolution."[15]

Even today, intellectuals who were themselves in the midst of the revolution are unsure what happened. "From [December] 16th to the 22nd, the fact is that the army killed the people," says writer Selian Tanase. "From the 22nd to the 25th, the army was still shooting, but we don't know who or why. I think platoons were shooting platoons."[16] But Radu Grozea, a former academic turned television producer, has a theory: "The shooting was organized by the army as a diversion on behalf of the winners—President Iliescu—to create the idea of a civil war."[17]

Others hypothesize that the army's motivation was not so much to bolster the new civilian leadership as to rehabilitate its own public image, which had been badly tarnished by the events in Timisoara. The staged battle against the terrorists—if that is what it was—had the additional benefit of further discrediting the Securitate, the army's long-time rival, which during Ceausescu's regime had come to eclipse the military in power and privilege.

Certain French journalists advanced yet another theory, one remarkably similar to Ceausescu's own: The revolution was a foreign plot devised by the Soviet Union. There is some intriguing evidence to support this theory. For example, a Soviet journalist claimed that there were nearly a dozen correspondents from TASS—the Soviet news agency that often served as cover for KGB agents—in Timisoara on December 10, five days *before* the protests began.[18] But while Moscow may indeed have had contacts with anti-Ceausescu conspirators dating back years, most observers agree that at best the Soviets were keenly interested observers of the Romanian revolution, not its godfather.

There is no doubt that elements in Romania's political and military elite had been plotting unsuccessfully against Ceausescu for years, and the NSF itself had been in existence for months before the revolution. In a videotape of the NSF's chaotic "founding meeting" on December 22, Nicolae Militaru, a retired army general, can be heard saying, "Hey guys, the National Salvation Front has been in action for six months, man!"[19]

Militaru was a key plotter and briefly served as defense minister of the new regime. In August 1990 he and Silviu Brucan went public in an interview in a Romanian newspaper with details of the long-standing anti-Ceausescu conspiracy. (Brucan, author of the famous "Letter of Six," had served as the NSF's ideologist and spokesman before having a falling out with Iliescu.) They said the plotting against Ceausescu had begun back in the mid-1970s, and that by the early 1980s the conspirators had settled on Iliescu as the best candidate to succeed the dictator. They said a coup had been set for 1984 but fizzled after news of it leaked.

Militaru and Brucan said that the plotters were caught by surprise by the Timisoara uprising but were able to take quick advantage of it due to their years of organizing. They gave full credit to the common people for launching the revolution, but added that "the idea that this 180-degree change [by the security forces] would have been made spontaneously is entirely mistaken . . . the dissident work within the army fully proved its political usefulness and its decisive role in preventing a bloody massacre in the whole country."[20]

Iliescu himself in 1990 said elliptically that "we may just as well speak of several conspiracies."[21] The question of whether the revolution was a genuine popular uprising or a coup, or an uprising cut short by a coup, continues to haunt Romanian politics to this day.

Most analysts agree that if not for the spontaneous bravery and righteous rage of the people in Timisoara and Bucharest, the revolution could not have succeeded. (At least, not at that time. Obviously Ceausescu could not have continued in power indefinitely.) On the other hand, the people alone could not have ousted the hated dictator if the army and Securitate had stuck by him. In some ways, the coup plotters can be seen as the short-term victors, for they are the ones who seized power and prevented a more complete and radical revolution from taking place that might have tried to eradicate all aspects of the old regime.

But, despite all the political squabbling that has taken place in the years since, it is undoubtedly the Romanian people who are the long-term victors. If only for a relatively brief moment, they were masters of their own destiny, and a crushing burden was lifted from the entire national consciousness. As one Romanian journalist who witnessed the revolution firsthand put it: "Frankly, I was surprised. I did not know we Romanians had it in us."[22]

NOTES

1. Mark Frankland, *The Patriots' Revolution*, p. 316.
2. Edward Behr, *Kiss the Hand You Cannot Bite*, pp. 247-248.
3. Nestor Ratesh, *Romania: The Entangled Revolution*, p. 28.
4. Frankland, op. cit., p. 310.
5. *Washington Post*, December 29, 1989.
6. Andrei Codrescu, *The Hole in the Flag*, p. 47.
7. Behr, op. cit., p. 26.
8. Ratesh, op. cit., p. 77.
9. Ratesh, op. cit., p. 52.
10. Codrescu, op. cit., p. 95.
11. Ibid, p. 108.
12. Ibid, p. 105.
13. Ibid, p. 103.
14. Ratesh, op. cit., pp. 63–64.
15. Ibid, p. 62.
16. Jane Perlez, *New York Times*, December 25, 1994.
17. Ibid.
18. Codrescu, op. cit., p. 171.
19. Ratesh, op. cit., p. 54.
20. Ibid, p. 86.
21. Ibid, p. 88.
22. Frankland, op. cit., p. 337.

PART II

ROMANIA TODAY

6

Government & Politics

T he history of Romanian politics in the years since the revolution is the story of a nation struggling to deal with the damaging legacy of Ceausescuism. To maintain himself in power, the dictator had successfully atomized the entire society, preventing any alternative power bases from arising to threaten his rule. So, unlike in other countries in Eastern Europe, no organized dissident groups were poised to step into the power vacuum once Ceausescu was toppled. "There was very little in terms of a counter-elite to create a real reform party," scholar Vladimir Tismaneanu notes. "That explains why you have the exit of Ceausescu and the entrance of Iliescu."[1]

This raises the issue of whether continued rule by Ion Iliescu's National Salvation Front (NSF), despite its various name changes over the years, represents what some have called post-Communist communism, or "neocommunism." This has been called "the paradox of the revolution: its having a clearly anticommunist character while 'legitimating' a government that is far from that."[2]

However, some observers find the neocommunism label misleading because the new leaders seem to be motivated not so much by ideology as by a desire to maintain power in a fragmented society unused to freedom. In this view, "if some of communism's structures remain, it is not because the leaders still want Marxism-Leninism but because those structures were eminently suited to concentrating political power and reproducing it."[3]

Although the government remains intolerant of dissent and has been slow to implement economic reforms, the situation in Romania today is light-years ahead of the darkness of the Ceausescu era. Romanians have a new constitution, an elected, multiparty parliament, independent unions, a lively press that is free (if not entirely independent), the right to travel and associate without restriction, and the right to express political views openly.

For all the economic hardship and political strife that have characterized Romania's transition to democracy, it is perhaps those last two rights that are the revolution's most tangible benefits for ordinary citizens. As a Romanian journalist recently said, "I have the right to an opinion which I can express freely, and I have the right to a passport which I couldn't dream of before."[4]

Elections and Unrest

The first two years of the new Romania was a chaotic period of rebuilding and unrest. The groundwork was gradually laid for a more democratic system, but before these new structures could establish stable roots, politics was exercised in a manner that could hardly be differentiated from street brawling.

Among its first actions in late 1989, the NSF changed the country's official name to simply Romania, dropping the title of "Socialist Republic"; declared an end to the constitutional monopoly on power by the Romanian Communist Party (RCP); canceled the destructive rural urbanization or "systemization" program; and promised early elections in 1990.

The honeymoon is over: In January 1990 in Bucharest, a protester against the new National Salvation Front government holds a sign equating communism and fascism. (AP/Wide World Photos)

Pending those elections, the country was initially ruled by a triumvirate: Iliescu as interim president, Dumitru Mazilu (a dissident former Securitate officer and diplomat) as interim vice-president, and Petre Roman (a youthful, 44-year-old engineering professor with no prior political background) as interim premier.

The new government's honeymoon was over within days. Large protests were staged in Bucharest in January 1990 demanding a purge of all Communists and the complete dismantling of the hated Securitate secret police. Startled, the NSF regime said it would outlaw the Romanian Communist Party, but it then went back on its word a few days later, saying such a move would be unconstitutional. (A smaller-version RCP was revived later in the year under a new name, the Socialist Labor Party.) The NSF also reversed its initial pledge not to participate in the forthcoming elections as a political party. The broken promises touched off new demonstrations and prompted Mazilu to resign in protest against the "Stalinist methods of the new leadership."

Just as in the revolution, the new protests were led by intellectuals and students. The NSF responded by mobilizing its own partisans, including factory workers who chanted the uninspired slogan: "We work; we don't think."[5] In late January, pro-government mobs ransacked the offices of the opposition National Peasants' Party and National Liberal Party, the two main parties of the prewar period that had been revived after the revolution.

As the unrest continued in February, the regime agreed to share power with the opposition in a Provisional National Unity Council in the run-up to the election, but the new body remained dominated by the NSF. At the request of the opposition, the voting was delayed for a month to allow more time for them to organize. It hardly helped: On May 20, in Romania's first free election in more than 50 years, the NSF won 65 percent of the seats in the new parliament, and Iliescu was elected president with 85 percent of the vote. More than 14 million of the country's 16 million eligible voters went to the polls.

International observers backed opposition claims of widespread voting irregularities, and there is no question that NSF supporters used intimidation, harassment, and other illegal tactics in the period leading up to the election and during the voting itself. But even allowing for vote-rigging and fraud, it was clear that the vast majority of Romanians—mostly conservative peasants and workers who did not share the views of the

Peasants and Gypsies line up in May 1990 to vote in Romania's first mostly free election in more than 50 years. (AP/Wide World Photos)

intellectual class—chose the continuity represented by the NSF, preferring the known to the unknown.

The election did little to bring political peace. Earlier in April, students had organized a permanent occupation of Bucharest's University Square, where tens of thousands of people gathered in what they declared a "Communist-free zone" to protest the government. After the election the crowds dwindled, but the encampment continued until mid-June, when police moved in and attacked the protesters with great brutality. That provoked an angry mob to march on government buildings and storm the television station.

With the police and army showing no willingness to confront the rioters, President Iliescu appealed to the working class to "save the democracy" from a "Fascist rebellion." On June 14, the government brought more than 10,000 coal miners from the Jiu Valley by train and truck into central Bucharest, where they were greeted by the president and then set loose to "restore order." Over the next two days the miners, armed with clubs and crowbars, savagely attacked and beat hundreds of students, Gypsies, and other perceived opponents and ransacked the offices of political opposition parties. The official death toll was six, with many serious injuries, while more than 1,000 people were detained. At a mass farewell rally June 15, Iliescu personally thanked the miners for "doing very good work," adding, "If I need you again, I will call you."[6]

The government-sanctioned violence drew strong international condemnation, and in protest the U.S. ambassador to Romania boycotted Iliescu's official inauguration as president in late June. The heavy-handed repression reinforced the view that Romania remained the least reformed of Eastern Europe's formerly Communist states and made it more difficult to attract foreign aid and trade.

The events of June 1990 in some ways remain as mysterious as those of December 1989. Opposition figures charged that the unrest had been orchestrated by "rogue" Securitate agents who first acted as provocateurs in the antigovernment riots and then directed some of the worst excesses of the miners. Analysts agree that the violence was a sign that the NSF was far from monolithic, and that opposing factions both inside and outside the government—including elements of both the army and the Securitate—were engaged in a shadowy, behind-the-scenes struggle for power.

The government of Premier Roman continued to be beset with large-scale protests against the country's deteriorating economy. The regime instituted some economic reforms, including limited privatization of state enterprises and the lifting of price controls. Reacting to the price increases, a new opposition movement, the Civic Alliance, staged a protest of 100,000 people in Bucharest in November 1990, and workers in Timisoara called a general strike the following month.

The popular protests did not let up in 1991. In September the Jiu Valley miners returned to Bucharest, but this time they came to confront the government. They demanded wage increases, a price freeze, and the resignation of both Iliescu and Roman. Joined by students and other antigovernment protesters (the same people the miners had beaten the previous year), the miners stormed the parliament and other government buildings, attacked the television station, and besieged the presidential palace. Violent clashes with security forces left at least four people dead.

The crisis forced Roman and his cabinet to resign. Iliescu appointed Theodor Stolojan, a former finance minister, as the new premier. Meanwhile, the conspiracy mill continued to churn. It was rumored that Iliescu had plotted with the miners to oust Roman (the president had begun to differ with his premier over the pace of economic reform). Others blamed the latest unrest, again, on the Securitate, or else on right-wingers seeking to topple the NSF.

The year ended on a more positive note when the parliament approved a new constitution in November and it was endorsed by 77 percent of voters in a national referendum in December. The new charter defined Romania as a multiparty presidential republic. It vested strong powers in the presidency, guaranteed human rights and ethnic diversity, and banned capital punishment and torture. The constitution also backed a free-market economy and the right to own private property, although it forbade foreigners from owning Romanian land.

There were further changes in the country's political landscape in 1992, but this time the changes were free of serious violence. In February and March the first post-Communist elections were held at the local level for seats on city and town councils. The voting confirmed a precipitous decline in the NSF's popularity: Its candidates won only about 33 percent of the races, a halving of its support from the 1990 national elections. The Democratic Convention of Romania (DCR), a newly formed alliance of 18 opposition parties from the political center-right, won nearly 25 percent of the seats. The DCR's strength was centered in major cities like Bucharest, Braso, Sibiu, Arad, and Timisoara, while the NSF ran stronger in rural areas.

The NSF Splits

The electoral setback led to a split in the NSF, as the feud between Roman and Iliescu erupted into the open. Following his forced resignation the previous fall, Roman had begun attacking the president, his former mentor, as a "neocommunist" opposed to reform. Iliescu responded by calling Roman a "political playboy" and a "political soldier of fortune"[7] who had betrayed the NSF's social democratic principles. In March 1992 there was a formal separation: Roman became president of the now centrist NSF while Iliescu and his followers split off to form the more leftist

Democratic National Salvation Front (DNSF)—which, since Iliescu was president, automatically became the ruling party.

Romania held its second post-revolution general election in September 1992. The DNSF won 28 percent of the seats in parliament, the DCR alliance about 20 percent and the NSF 10 percent, with the remaining seats split among five smaller parties. In the first round of the presidential voting, no candidate won more than 50 percent, necessitating a runoff between the two top finishers, Iliescu and Emil Constantinescu, a political novice endorsed by the DCR. In the second round of voting in October, Iliescu won with about 61 percent of the vote.

In the campaign Iliescu and the DNSF had taken advantage of the anxieties felt by farmers and workers in the transition to a free-market economy, labeling Constantinescu and the DCR as supporters of mass unemployment and "wild capitalism."[8] The DNSF also had the support of the *nomenklatura*, the former Communist bureaucrats and managers who still controlled much of the country's economy. Iliescu's critics charged that the DNSF was a haven for die-hard ex-Communists.

In November, Iliescu appointed, and the new parliament confirmed, Nicolae Vacaroiu as premier, replacing Stolojan, who had been in office only a year. Vacaroiu—an economist who opposed radical reform and called for a slower transition to capitalism—then assembled a cabinet that included equal numbers of DNSF members and independents.

In 1993, the ruling DNSF merged with three smaller left-wing parties to form the Party of Social Democracy in Romania (PSDR). Adrian Nastase was elected the party's executive chairman, while Iliescu remained the party's "moral guide," "patriarch," and "guru."[9] (Technically, the new Romanian constitution did not allow the country's president to be formally affiliated with any political party.) Meanwhile, Petre Roman's opposition NSF joined with the tiny Democratic Party and rechristened itself the Democratic Party-National Salvation Front (DP-NSF).

For Romania as a whole, 1993 was a "crucially uneventful year" marked by a "crisis of procrastination,"[10] and the same pattern persisted through 1994. Like many previous Romanian regimes, the current government achieved major diplomatic successes in its international relations (which will be covered in a later chapter), while at the same failing to make any real progress on pressing domestic issues, primarily regarding the stagnant economy.

Vacaroiu's minority PSDR government continued to defy predictions of its imminent demise. Despite corruption scandals and numerous attempts by the opposition to bring down the government through parliamentary motions of no-confidence, it somehow clung to power, owing in part to disunity among the opposition. By July 1994, it had survived five no-confidence votes, even though opinion polls showed that 74 percent of the public did not think it was doing a good job.

In some ways, the lack of dramatic developments in Romania in the 1993–94 period—reflected by the paucity of news coverage the country received in the international press—was a positive development. At least it indicated that Romania's civil society had matured to the point where it was no longer settling its political differences in the streets with clubs, guns, and riots. The main arena of conflict had switched to the ballot box and to the pages of the highly partisan free press.

There are limitations to Romania's freedom of the press, however. The powerful medium of television remains largely state-controlled, and the government holds a crucial monopoly on the supply of newsprint. In November 1994 the largest daily newspaper, *Evenimentul Zilei*, a sharp critic of the government, was forced to halve its 300,000 circulation after the state rationed its supply of paper.

The Rise of Extremism

One distinctly negative political development in the recent period has been the rise in power and influence of several extremist ultranationist parties. These include the Transylvania-based Party of Romanian National Unity, led by Gheorghe Funar, the mayor of Cluj; the Greater Romania Party, led by Corneliu Vadim Tudor; and the Socialist Labor Party (the former Communist Party). All three won parliamentary seats in the 1992 elections. They share similar traits: They are strongly anti-Semitic and anti-Hungarian, they blame foreigners (and their domestic "agents") for all of Romania's problems, and they advocate a policy of "radical continuity" with the national communism of the former Ceausescu dictatorship.

These parties represent a curious "red-brown" coalition (red being the symbolic color of communism and brown the color of fascism). Along with their nostalgia for Ceausescuism, the extremist parties have also been seeking to rehabilitate the reputation of Marshal Ion Antonescu, Romania's Fascist dictator during World War II. A statue honoring Antonescu was

A burnt-out Securitate building in Sibiu after the revolution. People are searching the rubble for any secret files that may have survived. (AP/Wide World Photos)

Facts on Iliescu

Romania's President Ion Iliescu was born on March 3, 1930, son of one of the few members of the prewar Romanian Communist Party. He became a leader of the Communist Youth Union as a teenager and was sent to Moscow in 1950 for training as a hydroelectric engineer. But he chose politics over a technical career, and with his impeccable Communist credentials he rose rapidly up the party ladder. By age 35 he was a member of the Central Committee and in 1967 he became minister for youth affairs. He was named Central Committee secretary in charge of ideology in 1971, but that same year he had a falling out with Ceausescu after accompanying him on his visit to China and North Korea.

Iliescu says the dictator "was literally fascinated by Korea . . . [It] was the perfect model of an absolute totalitarianism. On our return, he drew up a kind of platform for a cultural revolution Romanian style. That was the break."[11]

For his disagreement Iliescu was demoted to the provinces, but he gradually worked his way back to the party's Political Executive Committee later in the 1970s. In 1984 Ceausescu stripped him of all his party and government positions, perhaps because of suspicions that he was somehow involved in a purported coup plot that fizzled that year.

"I was somehow known as one who was not in Ceausescu's favor, because I used to express my opinions in a very direct way."[12] He ended up as director of the Bucharest State Technical Publishing House, a post he still held at the time of the 1989 revolution.

President Ion Iliescu.
(AP/Wide World Photos)

erected in the town of Slobozia in October 1993, and a government official attended the dedication ceremony, prompting a protest by the United States. As Andrei Codrescu said, "It is as if a statue of, let's say, the founder of the Ku Klux Klan were erected in Washington in a ceremony attended by Administration officials."[13]

In defending Antonescu, extremist leader Tudor told a Jewish historian: "If Antonescu had been a Hitler, you may rest assured that today we would not be watching you and [Chief Rabbi] Moses Rosen on the television screen in cultural programs but rather as ads for Palmolive, Camay . . . and other brands of soap."[14] (This was a sickening reference to the Nazi practice of using the remains of death camp victims to make soap.)

Such vicious rhetoric has become common in the nationalist press, and the extremist parties have been given extensive coverage on state-run television. President Iliescu has condemned the resurgence of anti-Semitism, but the ruling Party of Social Democracy in Romania has come to depend on the parliamentary support of these radical parties to remain in power. At first that cooperation was informal, but in August 1994 the Party of Romanian National Unity officially joined the government (among the cabinet posts it controlled was the justice ministry). Then, after months of haggling, in January 1995 the PSDR signed a protocol with the three main radical parties, formally cementing its alliance with the extremists in an arrangement popularly known as the "red quadrangle."[15]

PSDR Chairman Nastase admitted the new coalition was a "sensitive" issue that might harm Romania's image abroad, but he claimed that the extremists would now be forced to behave more responsibly. (As if to prove that was wishful thinking, the Party of Romanian National Unity promptly embarrassed the government by launching an anti-Semitic attack on Alfred Moses, the new U.S. ambassador to Bucharest.) Many observers see the regime's strategy—relying on extremists rather than building bridges to the moderate political opposition—as potentially disastrous for Romanian democracy.

Unsurprisingly, there have been reports that the rise of the extremist parties has been abetted by agents of the former Securitate. As of 1994, no fewer than nine different intelligence units were known to be operating in Romania. The main agency is the Romanian Intelligence Service, headed by Virgil Magureanu. In interviews he has claimed that his agency's personnel were carefully screened and that only a third of the 15,000 pre-revolution Securitate officers were offered employment in the new outfit.

Many Romanians remain suspicious of the continuing power of those associated with the worst excesses of the Securitate under the Ceausescu regime. These feelings were not alleviated by the special military tribunals held in 1990 and 1991 in which a number of Ceausescu loyalists, including high-ranking Securitate officers, were sentenced to long prison terms for ordering the shootings in Timisoara and Bucharest. Most of those sentences were later quietly reduced or even commuted under a general amnesty. Those let off lightly included Nicu Ceausescu, the dictator's son, who was given a 20-year sentence in September 1990 but freed in November 1992 on grounds of ill health.

No discussion of Romanian politics would be complete without mention of King Michael, who was forced to abdicate and flee into exile in Switzerland after the 1947 Communist takeover. In 1990, the king tried to visit Romania but was stopped at the airport by the new government. When he was finally permitted to visit in April 1992, he received a tumultuous welcome from thousands of Romanians in Bucharest. Perhaps because of that enthusiastic reception, the next time he tried to visit—in October 1994—the king was again denied entry at the airport. President Iliescu claimed that Michael, 74, represented a threat to "Romania's public constitutional order." But most Romanian analysts discounted any such threat, saying the basis of the king's popularity was purely nostalgic and emotional, not political.

NOTES

1. Jane Perlez, *New York Times*, December 25, 1994.
2. Ivo Banac, ed., *Eastern Europe in Revolution*, p. 125.
3. Ibid, p. 130.
4. Perlez, op. cit.
5. Nestor Ratesh, *Romania: The Entangled Revolution*, p. 130.
6. *Facts On File World News Digest*, June 22, 1990, p. 467A2.
7. Michael Shafir and Dan Ionescu, *RFE/RL*, January 1, 1993.
8. Ibid.
9. *RFE/RL*, August 27, 1993.
10. Michael Shafir and Dan Ionescu, *RFE/RL*, January 7, 1994.
11. Michael Shafir, *Transition*, April 14, 1995.
12. Ratesh, op. cit., p. 52.
13. Andrei Codrescu, *New York Times*, December 7, 1993.
14. Michael Shafir, *RFE/RL*, April 22, 1994.
15. Dan Ionescu, *RFE/RL*, July 29, 1994.

7

The People

As with many countries, Romania's sense of national identity is deeply influenced by issues of ethnicity, language, and culture. Although ethnic Romanians (those who speak Romanian as their first language and identify with Romanian culture) make up the vast majority of the population, they often define themselves as much by who they are *not*—i.e., Hungarians, Jews, etc.—as by who they *are*.

The collapse of communism has let the nationalist genie out of the bottle all over Eastern Europe. Ethnic differences that had been suppressed by strict government control of all aspects of life have once again taken center stage. Ethnic groups tend to have long historical memories and to nurse grudges against other groups that can date back centuries. Communist rule merely kept these problems hidden below the surface, where they continued to fester like an untreated wound. As one Hungarian journalist considering the Transylvania question has said, "In East Europe we all feel guilty, and we all point the finger at someone else."[1]

In this respect, the problems Romania has faced since the revolution are no worse than many of those that have arisen in other Eastern European states. Indeed, after observing the ethnic and religious civil wars that have ripped apart neighboring Yugoslavia, it is amazing that Romania's group relations have remained as peaceful as they have, considering the country's complicated history.

Before going any further into Romania's ethnic situation, it will be useful to look at some basic statistics concerning the country's population and demographics. According to the January 1992 census, Romania had a

Scenes of rural life in Romania sometimes seem to be from an earlier time. This old woman is carrying her load in the village of Uzunu. (AP/Wide World Photos)

population of 22,760,449. Of that total, 20,408,542 (89.4 percent) are Romanians and 2,401,493 (10.6 percent) are members of ethnic minorities. The latter break down as follows: 7.1 percent Hungarians (Magyars and Szeklers), 1.7 percent Gypsies (although that may be a significant undercount), 0.5 percent Germans (Saxons and Swabians), 0.3 percent Ukrainians, and 0.04 percent Jews. The remainder consists of Serbians, Croats, Russians, Czechs, Slovaks, Slovenes, Bulgarians, Turks, and Tartars. An estimated 8 million Romanians live outside the national boundaries, most of them in Moldova, Ukraine, Hungary, Albania, Bulgaria, and Yugoslavia.

The religious makeup consists of 86.8 percent Romanian Orthodox, 5.3 percent Roman Catholic (Hungarians and Germans), and 3.5 percent Reformed or Calvinist (mostly Hungarians). The rest consists mainly of various Protestant churches, including Lutheran, Pentecostal, Baptist, and Evangelical, as well as Muslims. Jews are officially counted as an ethnic rather than a religious group.

The country's average population density is 95.7 inhabitants per square mile. The population density is heaviest in central and southwestern Walachia and central and northwestern Transylvania. The population concentrated in urban areas amounts to 54.3 percent, a significantly lower percentage than elsewhere in Europe. This distribution of the population is illustrated by the fact that while Bucharest has more than 2 million inhabitants, the next seven largest cities—Constanta, Iasi, Timisoara, Cluj-Napoca, Galati, Brasov, and Craiova—have populations of 350,000 or less.

Most of the areas of the Old Kingdom (Walachia and Moldavia) continue to be ethnically homogeneous, with many districts essentially 100 percent inhabited by Romanians. Among the exceptions are northern Moldavia and Bukovina, which until World War II had significant numbers of Jews; Dobruja, where there is a large percentage of Bulgarians, Russians, Tartars, and Turks; and Bucharest, which has large Hungarian and Gypsy communities.

But clearly the most ethnically heterogeneous regions of Romania are Transylvania and the Banat (the two areas are often lumped together). This area is home to most of Romania's Hungarian- and German-speaking population. More than 20 percent of Transylvania's people are Hungarian.

The Hungarian Question

The long history behind the dispute between Romanians and Hungarians in Transylvania has been covered in detail in earlier chapters. What follows is an account of how that struggle has manifested itself in the years since the 1989 revolution.

Following Ceausescu's overthrow, Hungarian activists began demanding greater use of the Hungarian language in education and on street signs. Romanian ultranationalists responded by organizing a quasi-Fascist organization, *Vatra Romaneasca* (Romanian Cradle, or Hearth), and its political arm, the Party of Romanian National Unity (PRNU). When Hungarians staged a demonstration in the town of Tirgu Mures in March 1990 they were violently attacked by a mob of Romanian extremists, sparking two days of riots in which five people were killed (three Romanians and two Hungarians) and troops were called out to restore order.

In a bid for the support of the ultranationalists, the new National Salvation Front government placed all the blame for the incident on the Hungarians, whom President Iliescu labeled "hooligans." His foreign minister claimed, "It is not the NSF that has alienated the Hungarian minority. The Hungarian minority has decided to alienate itself from the NSF."[2] In subsequent general elections, the Hungarian Democratic Federation of Romania (HDFR) became a significant opposition force in the national parliament.

Tensions worsened after a leading Romanian extremist, Gheorghe Funar, was elected mayor of the city of Cluj in February 1992. (He later became leader of the Party of Romanian National Unity.) He immediately began a campaign to expunge the Hungarian language from public use, beginning with the removal of the city's bilingual street signs. Later in the year, ethnic Hungarian prefects in two Transylvanian districts were replaced by Romanians, and the only Hungarian state secretary in the national government lost his post. In 1993 the government sought to ease tensions by signing an agreement on minority rights that supposedly provided for the training of Hungarian-speaking schoolteachers and guaranteed bilingual street signs in areas with a Hungarian population of at least 30 percent.

However, attempts to "Romanize" the Hungarian minority continued to gain ground throughout the country in 1994, worsening relations between Romania and Hungary. Extremist parties helped push a bill through the lower house of parliament that would ban church-sponsored Hungarian language schools. Laszlo Tokes, the Hungarian pastor who helped spark the Timisoara uprising in December 1989, said the new law was "totally discriminatory, worse than in the times of Ceausescu."[3]

Meanwhile, Funar sponsored an archaeological dig in Cluj's main square that, although ostensibly aimed at finding the ruins of an ancient Roman forum, would coincidentally also require the removal of a statue of Hungary's 15th-century King Mathias. Thousands of Hungarians rallied to block the start of the excavation. "That statue embodies our community consciousness and our history," Tokes said. "It's the symbol of our struggle for rights in the face of 75 years of humiliation."[4]

On the other side, Cluj deputy prefect and Party of Romanian National Unity member Liviu Medrea declared: "In Romania, the time has passed when those belonging to an ethnic minority group can dictate to us . . . We are sure that truth and right are on our side."[5]

Exodus

Although most of Romania's ethnic Hungarians showed every sign of staying put, many other Romanians have continued to vote with their feet and flee the country as both political and economic refugees. In the latter years of Ceausescu's rule, Romania had become "a foremost supplier of refugees to other countries."[6] The flood of emigrants grew even larger after the revolution, with thousands swarming into Western Europe, particularly Germany. By late 1993, one-quarter of all those seeking asylum in Germany were from Romania (many of them Gypsies).

One survey estimated that 250,000 Romanian citizens had sought asylum abroad between 1990 and 1993. Another 1.5 million Romanians—most of them young and well-educated—were said to be considering emigration.

Not all of the Romanian exodus was haphazard or unplanned. During the 1980s, the West German government had paid the Ceausescu regime large sums to allow tens of thousands of ethnic Germans to return to their motherland. The process continued after the revolution, and in 1990 an

The Plight of the Gypsies

Two-thirds of Europe's 8 million Gypsies live in Central and Eastern Europe, with Romania having the largest concentration of all. (The 1992 census put Romania's total at around 400,000, but many experts consider that a serious underestimate, whether deliberate or otherwise. Some put the real number at around 2 million.) In their own language Gypsies prefer to call themselves Roma, although that has nothing to do with Romania; they are descendants of a people who first reached Europe in the 11th century after a long migration from India. Traditionally they are a nomadic people who live in rural encampments and move from place to place, supporting themselves with temporary menial work and sometimes with illegal activities, although many have settled in cities and hold regular jobs.

Just as the fall of communism has unleashed latent currents of anti-Semitism across Eastern Europe, so has it sharpened widespread public hostility toward Gypsies. They "are generally persecuted by the police, humiliated by the local authorities and made to live on the margin," one Romanian human rights activist says. "There is a large campaign to present Gypsies all the time as criminals, in the press and television, and this is perpetuated by teachers. This is a tragedy of our schools."[7]

In 1991 there were organized attacks on Gypsy communities throughout Romania, prompting thousands to flee the country, mostly to Germany. (In September 1992 the German government sent 43,000 Romanian refugees, more than half of them Gypsies, back to Romania after agreeing to pay millions of dollars for their resettlement.) The attacks continued over the next two years, and after almost every incident the authorities arrested only Gypsies, blaming them for provoking the clashes.

One of the worst occurred in the Transylvanian village of Hadreni in September 1993 after a large gang attacked four young Gypsy men. One of

estimated 120,000 members of Romania's German-speaking community (known as Saxons and Swabians) immigrated to Germany.

The Jewish exodus was even more complete. The Israeli government had also paid Ceausescu to allow the mass immigration of Romania's Jews to Israel. Of the 400,000 Jews who survived the Romanian Holocaust, all but 20,000 had left by 1989. That number continued to dwindle still further as anti-Semitism mounted in Romania after the revolution. By the time of the Romanian attackers was stabbed to death, after which hundreds of villagers set fire to the house in which the Gypsies had taken refuge and then killed three of them as they tried to escape the flames. The mob then burned and destroyed more than a dozen Gypsy homes. No arrests were made. The deputy mayor, asked if the Gypsies could ever forget what had happened, replied: "We hope they will. They know it was their fault."[8]

A more positive development came in May 1994 when Gypsy representatives from 14 European countries staged a four-day unity conference in Snagov, Romania, at which they called for full human rights and planned self-help projects and an information center to document anti-Gypsy violence. The conference was cosponsored by an American group and the Romanian government, representing the first time any European government had given official recognition to the Gypsy community as a "transnational non-territorial minority."

A Gypsy family walks through Sibiu's old district in April 1993. This is a sign of progress, as in the past the police would have kept Gypsies out of the neighborhood entirely. (AP/Wide World Photos)

the January 1992 census, the number of Jews remaining in the country was put at only 8,955.

Rhetorical attacks on Jews in Romania—and in Eastern Europe generally—often take the form of blaming the Jews for communism. While Jews had played a disproportionate role in the early days of the Romanian Communist Party, virtually all of them were later purged from power, a process finished by Ceausescu in the 1970s. "Most of these fanatical Jewish communists ended up in Israel after they were thrown out of their jobs," according to Romania's Chief Rabbi Moses Rosen. "Now they're all big Zionists."[9]

NOTES

1. Mark Frankland, *The Patriots' Revolution*, p. 339.
2. Gale Stokes, *The Walls Came Tumbling Down*, p. 174.
3. David B. Ottaway, *Washington Post*, July 5, 1994.
4. Ibid.
5. Ibid.
6. Michael Shafir, *RFE/RL*, June 24, 1994.
7. Henry Kamm, *New York Times*, November 17, 1993.
8. Henry Kamm, *New York Times*, October 27, 1993.
9. Charles Hoffman, *Gray Dawn*, p. 131.

8

The Economy

*R*omanians could forgive their government a multitude of political sins as long as it delivered on its basic promises of ensuring economic stability and growth. So far, these pledges remain mostly unfulfilled. The 1990–93 period was marked by stagnant or negative growth, declining incomes, high inflation, labor unrest, and food shortages. There were some positive signs in 1994 that the government was beginning to get its fiscal house in order: Inflation was tamed, the deficit began to shrink, and exports improved markedly. But these modest gains meant little to the average Romanian citizen.

Estimates of the number of people living below the official poverty line—a monthly income of $160 for a family of four—ranged from 20 percent to 50 percent. Most households spent more than 70 percent of their income on food. Meanwhile, the impoverished masses could observe, with mixed envy and resentment, the small segment of the newly wealthy who flaunted their foreign cars and expensive clothes and dined at expensive restaurants in Bucharest. Most of these nouveaux riches

*A woman worker
wears a gas mask
during a break
from her job at a
nonferrous metals
plant in Copsa
Mica. Some 300,000
tons of aerial pollut-
ants pour out of the
town's two factories
each year, among
the worst rates in
Eastern Europe.*
(AP/Wide World
Photos)

seemed to be well-placed members of the former Communist Party who
had been able to make small fortunes trading on their insider contacts
with the government establishment.

"It's a period of searching and we haven't found the way," said one
middle-aged widow. "The people in power keep us going backward
because they are afraid of losing their political and economic advan-
tages."[1] She added that she was glad communism was gone even though
her living standards were worse than they had been under the Ceausescu
dictatorship.

Some basic facts about the Romanian economy: In 1993, the last year for which firm figures are available, the country's gross domestic product (GDP) registered a slight increase over 1992. That represented a distinct improvement, as in 1992 the GDP had plummeted 16 percent from its 1991 level. In 1993 industry made up 54.4 percent of the GDP, agriculture contributed 21.9 percent, and services accounted for 23.7 percent.

Industrial production increased by 1.3 percent in 1993 after having fallen between 15 percent and 20 percent in 1992. The manufacturing sector consists mainly of iron and steel making, chemicals, mechanical engineering, and timber-processing. These industries have been badly affected by shortages of electricity and raw materials. Coal, iron ore, and salt are the major mining products. Onshore petroleum production continues to decline, although it has been supplemented by new offshore platforms in the Black Sea. The strapped energy sector depends on petroleum, natural gas, coal, and hydroelectric power. Plans for Romania's first nuclear power plant have been indefinitely postponed.

Agricultural production grew 12 percent in 1993 following a 12 percent decline in 1992 caused by a severe drought. The principal crops are corn (maize), wheat, barley, sugar beet, potatoes, grapes, cabbages, and tomatoes. Wine production, forestry, and fisheries are significant contributors as well.

One of the most promising service sectors is tourism, where the potential for future growth appears to be great. Romanian operators have been aggressively marketing tour packages that include Black Sea coast resorts, the country's world-famous health spas, and "Dracula tourism"—following in the footsteps of Vlad the Impaler. However, the country's tourist infrastructure (hotels and restaurants) remains woefully underdeveloped and greatly in need of foreign investment.

Romania's main source of imports and main market for exports through 1991 was the Soviet Union. The dissolution in that year of both the U.S.S.R. and the Soviet-dominated Council for Mutual Economic Assistance (CMEA, or Comecon) put a major crimp in Romania's balance of trade situation. Hoped-for trade with Western nations has yet to fill the gap.

A succession of Romanian governments implemented a number of price liberalization or subsidy elimination programs between 1991 and 1993. These resulted in massive increases in the cost of staple goods, energy, and basic services that seriously affected the standard of living and prompted widespread social unrest, including waves of strikes and demonstrations. The price shocks, combined with the addition of a value-added tax in July 1993, led to a 24 percent decline in retail sales.

Rising prices also helped feed ravenous inflation rates of 230 percent in 1991, 211 percent in 1992, and 255 percent in 1993. The country's currency, the leu ("lion"; plural: lei), continued to fall sharply. By October 1993 it had crossed the "psychological threshold" of 1,000 lei to the U.S. dollar at the official exchange rate, while on the black market a dollar was already fetching 1,800 lei.

However, the reformists in the government of Premier Nicolae Vacaroiu held firm, and the tide gradually began to turn in 1994. The central bank tightened the money supply, lending less and sharply increasing the interest rate, and in April the leu was "floated" (became internally convertible with other currencies). As a result the leu was stabilized, inflation shrank from a monthly average of 12 percent to less than 6 percent, and investment and exports picked up briskly.

This progress impressed Romania's foreign creditors, led by the International Monetary Fund (IMF), which agreed to advance Romania its first new loan in nearly two years. The $700 million loan was tied to a Romanian commitment to reduce its budget deficit to below 3 percent of GDP and its annual inflation to 30 percent or less. (In 1994 those figures stood at 3.5 percent and 62 percent, respectively.) But most Romanians were still waiting impatiently for the benefits of such macroeconomic reforms to "trickle down" to their level.

Plodding Privatization

After the 1989 revolution, international humanitarian aid poured into Romania. But Western governments, banks, and businesses made it clear that large-scale financial aid and foreign investment for Romania would depend on the country completely restructuring its state-run command economy into a free market economy with large-scale private ownership. With support from the IMF, the World Bank, and other major lenders, the government established the National Agency for Privatization in August 1990 and enacted further laws in 1991 calling for the sell-off of state-owned enterprises to be completed within seven years.

In the years that followed, however, the privatization program has proceeded at a pace that can charitably be called glacial and that lags far behind the rest of Eastern Europe. Although Romania has one of the most industrialized economies in the region, most of it remains in state hands. As a result, by late 1993 Romania had attracted a total of only $600 million in foreign investment. This compares to $5 billion invested in neighboring Hungary, which has only half of Romania's population but a much more developed capitalist economy.

There has been some progress. As of 1994, the private sector accounted for 31 percent of Romania's GDP and provided 41 percent of its employment. But virtually all of that came from small-scale privatization in agriculture and the service sector; the dominant industrial sector remained almost untouched. Of the 6,000 state enterprises earmarked under the program, only 8 percent had been sold to the private sector. One senior

A computer-assembly plant. Romania's work force is well-educated, but its factories need foreign investment if they are to modernize. (AP/Wide World Photos)

official has been quoted as saying, "Reform in Romania continually starts off in spring and dies off in autumn with the cold weather, when it falls back into the paralyzing sleep of hibernation."[2]

There are a number of reasons for the delays. The cadres of state managers and bureaucrats, the so-called *nomenklatura,* are competing for control of the privatization drive. Most of them have little incentive to speed up the process, which might result in their losing influence or even their jobs. In addition, the ruling minority government, the leftist Party of Social Democracy in Romania (PSDR), has been accused of creating new bureaucratic hurdles to privatization under the excuse of streamlining the process. President Ion Iliescu, Premier Vacaroiu, and the PSDR as a whole depend on the support of the *nomenklatura* and the votes of workers in state-run factories. Many economically nonviable plants might be closed, resulting in massive layoffs if privatization went ahead.

"The government is slow on privatization because it represents the big industries," according to Dan Pascariu, chairman of the Romanian Bank of Commerce. "The government still thinks of restructuring as a political concept rather than an economic or business one."[3]

The government's fear of offending key industrial sector workers is not without basis. The coal miners from the Jiu Valley have marched on Bucharest several times since their first violent foray there in support of the government in 1990. In 1991 they successfully ousted Premier Petre Roman, and in 1993 they staged a strike that nearly brought down Vacaroiu's government. The uneconomical mining operations received heavy government subsidies, and the miners were among Romania's best-paid workers. "If today the government says it is shutting down the mines, tomorrow we will be back on the streets of Bucharest," warned one miners' union leader.[4]

Mixed Agricultural Reforms

Unlike the industrial sector, the nation's agricultural system did undergo significant privatization in the early 1990s. However, the reforms did not achieve as much success initially as had been anticipated in terms of increased production. Indeed, by the end of 1992, Romania—one of the most fertile countries in Europe—had reached the "embarrassing" point of having to import much of its food, according to its minister of agriculture.[5] There were numerous reasons for the slow progress: Legal uncertainties continued to deter new investment; fragmented land redistribution led to inefficient farming practices; and there was a persistent shortage of machinery and labor.

Under communism, the government ran 95 percent of all farming activity. It was divided between large state-run farms and smaller cooperatives, both of which had access to machine and tractor stations and a single supply and distribution network. After the revolution, members of the cooperatives were given provisional ownership certificates and offered various options regarding how they wished to farm.

By the end of 1992, it was estimated that 13 percent of the land was controlled by state farms, 13 percent by incorporated agricultural societies, 12 percent by unincorporated associations, 17 percent by communal (public) ownership, and 45 percent by individual farmers. But around 75 percent of the tractors remained owned by tractor stations and state farms, leaving inadequate equipment for the vast majority of farmers. There was only one tractor for every 62 new landowners and one truck for every 405 small farmers, and each plow had to be shared by a dozen people.

The results are readily apparent in the Romanian countryside. As one foreign journalist wrote in mid-1994:

> Along the 100 miles from Artand on the Hungarian border to Cluj farmers could be seen cutting and stacking hay and hauling it to their barns. No one was using machinery, just scythes and wooden pitchforks—pastoral, picturesque and utterly pre-industrial . . . Not a single tractor was seen along the Artand-Cluj road. Cows were a rare sight, which apparently explains why there is no fresh milk at the Continental Hotel [in Cluj].[6]

Another problem is the growing labor shortage, as the long-term migration of young people from rural to urban areas continues. One survey of more than 500 villages found that 59 percent of Romania's farm workers are now over 60 years old, while only 8.9 percent are under 40.

The government is open about admitting to the problems and trying to devise solutions. So far, it has sought most of all to keep the price of agricultural production under control to protect urban consumers. But 45

*A farmer waits for a buyer for his potatoes at an agricultural market in
Popesti. Privatization of Romanian agriculture has so far yielded mixed
results.* (AP/Wide World Photos)

percent of the population still live in rural areas, and there is a growing recognition in Bucharest that the urban-rural balance now has to be shifted back in favor of the farmers if the potentially great riches of Romanian agriculture are to be realized.

The Caritas Scheme

One of the more amazing economic stories of post-revolutionary Romania revolves around the so-called Caritas Affair. Caritas began as a "mutual aid" society in the Transylvanian city of Brasov and then moved its operations to Cluj in June 1992. Devised by an accountant, Ioan Stoica, it promised investors an eightfold return on their money within three months. It thus appeared to be a classic pyramid scheme (also known as a Ponzi scheme), in which the money of new investors is used to pay back earlier investors rather than for any legitimate money-making enterprise. But the supply of funds cannot rise exponentially forever, and eventually all such scams collapse of their own weight, leaving the early investors rich and the later ones bankrupt.

Many Romanians, confronted with high inflation and low bank interest rates, cared little about such matters. In the first nine months of 1993, despite warnings from the government, an estimated 3 million to 4 million Romanians (a fifth of the adult population) invested $1 billion in the get-rich-quick scheme, a sum equal to half of the government's annual budget. Thousands of people from around the country descended on Cluj in what was termed "mass psychosis," "chaos," and "a new El Dorado."[7]

Aside from Stoica and other early investors, many of whom became millionaires, the other main beneficiary was Gheorghe Funar, mayor of Cluj and leader of the extremist Party of Romanian National Unity (PRNU), who was an early and ardent backer of Caritas. As a result, his city and party received a huge influx of funds as well as massive media attention, all of which served Funar's ambitions to expand the PRNU from its Transylvanian base into a truly national party.

Caritas failed to pay out substantial returns to investors from November 1993 onward. But predictions of a social explosion in the wake of the scheme's gradual collapse proved unfounded. Many investors reportedly blamed the failure on the government, the central bank, and the news

The Coca-Cola Revolution

The Coca-Cola Company has provided one of the brightest spots in the Romanian economy during the transition period. In early 1990 it became one of the first foreign firms to invest in the country. By the beginning of 1995 Coke had invested a total of $150 million (out of a total of $1.5 billion in Eastern Europe) to create local bottlers and a sales and distribution system for its famous soft drink. In a three-year period Romanians went from drinking no Coke to an average of 47 eight-ounce servings a year, the fastest growth rate in company history.

More importantly, a study by an American business college found that "a minimum of 23,900 jobs was supported by the sale of Coca-Cola products in the Romanian retail sector."[8] For each job that Coke created directly, 11 jobs were created elsewhere in the economy, and "as many as 20,000 to 25,000 kiosks and other small retail shops started or maintained their business because of Coca-Cola." This was helping to form a base for free-market activity and to create a new class of small-scale entrepreneurs—the hated "petty bourgeoisie" of Marxist jargon.

"Our system always guaranteed that we got second-rate products, so there was no pride in what we sold," one storekeeper says. "Then Coke comes in with its new trucks and new bottles and its drivers in new uniforms. Everything is high quality. That makes us feel better about ourselves."

media rather than on Stoica or Funar. (Stoica was finally arrested in August 1994.)

Many observers were surprised that the scam lasted as long as it did. Speculation swirled as to who or what provided the "deep pockets" behind Caritas, which some suspected was in fact a gigantic, criminal money-laundering operation (in which "dirty" money is "cleaned" by being cycled through legitimate channels). The possible culprits mentioned in Romanian news accounts included the Romanian Intelligence Service (RIS), the Italian Mafia, or Eastern European organized crime gangs. Some suggested that the money behind Caritas originated from international drug-trafficking or illegal arms sales to various sides of the Yugoslavian civil wars.[9]

Romanians do not seem to suffer from the fear of "Coca-colonization" at the hands of multinational corporations that is common in some foreign countries. "There is not the feeling in Romania of being exploited by multinationals," according to a government economist. "Rather, people see multinationals as a vehicle for transferring organizational and managerial skills."

Wine Before Its Time

A less inspiring story involves an indigenous Romanian beverage: wine. Romanians consume an average of more than 40 bottles per person annually, twice the rate of Britain. The country has one of the best climates in the world for wine-growing, and some of its vintages are world famous. Romania is the world's eighth-largest wine producer—making 600 million liters (150 million gallons) a year—but exports only 4 percent of that total. By comparison, post-Communist Hungary exports 40 percent of its wine production, while Bulgaria exports 70 percent.

One problem is that, although most Romanian vineyards are now privately owned, they lack the capital and foreign investment needed for expansion due to a legal ban on foreigners owning land. That may change, but not soon enough to suit the nation's winegrowers. "We are in a transition period from a very stupid government to a medium-stupid government," says Viorel Stoian, head of the National Wine Institute. "Meanwhile, our vineyards are deteriorating."[10]

NOTES

1. Jane Perlez, *New York Times*, November 24, 1993.
2. Don Ionescu, *Transition*, April 14, 1995.
3. Ibid.
4. Roger Thurow, *Wall Street Journal*, October 20, 1994.
5. David C. Henry, *RFE/RL*, February 18, 1994.
6. David B. Ottaway, *Washington Post*, August 1, 1994.
7. Michael Shafir, *RFE/RL*, September 24, 1993.
8. Ibid., pp. 25-27.
9. Nathaniel C. Nash, *New York Times*, February 26, 1995. All subsequent quotes in Chapter 8, except the last, come from this article.
10. Nathaniel C. Nash, *New York Times*, March 8, 1995.

9

Daily Life

*T*he transition to democracy and a free-market economy has been rough for most Romanians. There is no doubt that the new political freedoms and the ending of the most totalitarian aspects of communism under Ceausescu—such as the constant surveillance by the Securitate and the ban on abortions and birth control—have made daily life less psychologically oppressive and easier to bear. But most Romanians, like people all over the world, are preoccupied with day-to-day concerns: safe streets, decent housing, health care, and feeding their families. By these basic yardsticks, the quality of life in Romania has shown either no improvement or only a marginal advantage since the 1989 revolution.

Public opinion surveys conducted in Romania from late 1991 to early 1993 indicate a growing dissatisfaction with the current transitional period. While most people favor privatization and free markets in principle, they are increasingly coming to resent the social costs they are being forced to bear. Indeed, a significant minority are either becoming "nostalgic" for the

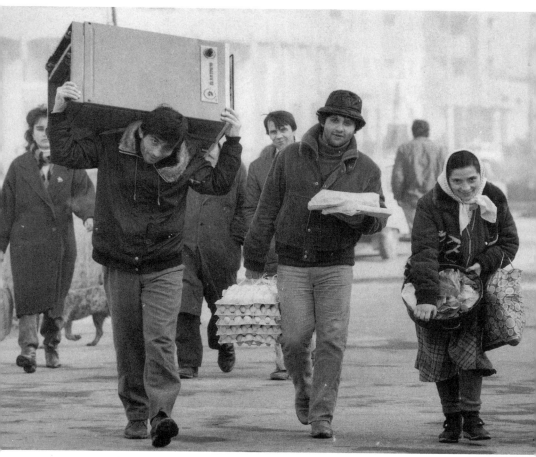

Romanian shoppers return home with food and a washing machine; the cost of the latter equaled one to two months' wages. (AP/Wide World Photos)

Communist era or at least beginning to think that life under Ceausescu was perhaps not so terrible after all.[1]

Winters remain the hardest time of year. The government is sensitive to comparisons of the present period to the notorious "Ceausescu winters" of the 1980s, when the heat was often turned off and people froze in their dimly lit apartments. Bucharest residents in 1993 said their homes were no longer as cold as that, although they admitted to often wearing their overcoats inside.

On paper, Romania has a comprehensive social welfare system. Government- and employer-funded insurance schemes provide for health

Constantin Surescu, 70, stands in front of his former home in Cornetu outside Bucharest, holding a picture of what it used to look like. It was razed as part of Ceausescu's rural "systemization" policy. (AP/Wide World Photos)

care, sickness benefits, children's allowances, unemployment payments, and pensions. But such benefits were not adequate to cope with the huge price increases in basic goods and services that occurred in the early 1990s as the government ended many subsidies.

Food remained the biggest concern for most people. Although there were some actual shortages—sugar and dairy products, for example—in most cases food was available on the free market but was often priced beyond the reach of the average Romanian. This caused a steady decline in consumption in 1992 of such things as fresh meat, fish, eggs, and fruit, putting Romania well below other former Communist countries like Bulgaria, Hungary, and Poland.

Housing remains another problem. Under Ceausescu, the government built dreary high-rise apartment complexes for workers in urban areas. Most of these were shoddily built and have not aged well, but the new post-Communist government has not had the funds to replace them and the struggling free market in construction has not taken up the slack.

The coal miners of the Jiu Valley town of Petrosani are supposedly among Romania's more privileged workers, earning a higher salary than most. But "we live like pigs," one miner told a foreign journalist, showing off a dank, tiny four-room apartment shared by two families of seven people. The story does not end there, though:

> A neighbor, a miner's wife, claims her apartment is worse and confidently opens her door. There are no light switches on the walls; live wires simply dangle from holes in the concrete. She turns on a light by gingerly wrapping two wires together. There is no hot water, and to take a bath is to flirt with death. The woman produces a primitive homemade water heater, a crude copper coil stretched between two sticks of wood, that she connects to one of the loose wires and tosses into the water. "If I even touch the bathtub like this," she says, extending a finger, "I'll be electrocuted."[2]

There are some bright spots on the housing scene, however. Some Romanians are rebuilding the homes that were demolished as part of Ceausescu's "systemization" (rural urbanization) scheme. Under that much-hated program, many villagers' houses were bulldozed and their owners forced to move into dormitory-style apartment complexes. Today

The Orphan Story

Romanians are a proud people, and so they often find themselves discouraged and embarrassed that the only thing many Americans seem to know about their country (aside from vampire stories) is the sad tale of its orphans. Perhaps that is not too surprising, because—as one scholar has written—"The discovery after 1989 of orphanages filled with thousands of wretched children living in medieval filth was the single most horrible revelation to come out of any formerly communist country in Eastern Europe."[3]

Many of these children were not technically orphans, for they had been abandoned after their mothers were forced to give birth to them (Ceausescu having banned abortions and contraception in a mad effort to increase the population). It was subsequently discovered that as many as one baby in every four was infected with AIDS due to contaminated blood injections. The orphans' plight was widely publicized in the West, and many foreign couples traveled to Romania in the immediate aftermath of the revolution to arrange quick, if legally questionable, adoptions.

One traveler who visited an orphanage in the early 1990s wrote movingly of being surrounded by children as she left: "'When will my mother come? Whose mother are you?' they keep asking. One of them puts his arm through mine, and walks with me toward the gate with the look of the purest sadness and supplication I've ever seen in human eyes."[4]

Western couples, working through callous local lawyers and Gypsy middlemen, often paid substantial sums of money to bypass orphanages and adopt an infant directly from the child's parents. The Romanian government, concerned about their country's growing reputation as a source of black-market babies, cracked down and passed a law in 1991 placing new restrictions on foreign adoptions. A British couple was arrested in July 1994 on charges of trying to smuggle an illegally adopted baby out of the country. They were sentenced to more than two years in jail but were freed in November and ordered to leave Romania.

in the village of Vladiceasca, near Bucharest, the new local authorities are allowing residents to return to their old homesteads.

Standing outside the quaint house he had rebuilt on his reclaimed property, a villager recalled, "I would weep every day I went by here on the bus to work. They said they pulled our houses down to make

Estimates of the number of children still living in institutions range from 50,000 to 80,000, many of whom are physically, mentally, or emotionally disabled. Today a growing number of civic-minded Romanians are working with their local government and churches to encourage adoption and foster care within the country and to start smaller, family-oriented group homes that provide a more loving atmosphere for children than large orphanages. "The children in these [state-run] institutions are like shells, and the more the vagaries of life wash over them, the more they close up," says the director of one of the new private group homes. "In a family surrounding, they just open up."[5]

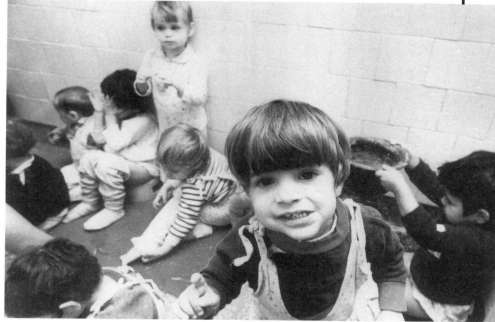

One of the poignant images of Romania's orphans that gripped the world's attention in the early 1990s. (AP/Wide World Photos)

use of the land for agriculture. But they didn't do anything with it. It just lay fallow."[6]

"We belong here, we have something that belongs to us," he said proudly. "We couldn't live like anonymous people in those blocks of flats."

The Health Crisis

An even more telling example of the Ceausescu legacy is demonstrated by Romania's continuing health care crisis. By most statistical indicators the situation has gotten steadily worse since the 1989 revolution, a reflection of both the deteriorating economy and "health hazards accumulated during the communist era."[7] These include environmental pollution, a shortage of medicines, and unheated homes in winter.

In 1992 the nation's population actually decreased by 3,462, the first time that had happened in modern Romanian history outside of wartime. Two major factors were increased emigration and the ending two years before of Ceausescu's "pro-birth" policies, which had banned abortion and contraceptives. The end of those restrictions caused the ratio of abortions to births to explode: It was three to one in 1990–91, one of the highest such rates in the world. The introduction of more progressive, Western family-planning practices lowered the ratio to 2.6 to 1 in the 1992–93 period.

Life expectancy in Romania is among the lowest in Europe: 69.5 years in 1991 (73 for women; 66 for men), down from 71 in 1989. From 1991 to 1992 the death rate per 1,000 inhabitants rose from 10.9 to 11.6, while the birth rate fell from 11.9 to 11.4, the lowest level in this century. Perhaps most worrisome of all, the infant mortality rate (measuring the number of babies who die before their first birthday) continued to rise, reaching 23.4 deaths per 1,000 infants in 1992, a rate in Europe second only to Albania. (The average rate for Europe, including former Communist countries, was just over 10 per 1,000.)

Various communicable diseases are also on the rise. Tuberculosis—known as the "squalor disease" because it is spread by unsanitary living conditions—climbed steadily from 64 people per 1,000 in 1990 to 92.7 in the first quarter of 1993. Contaminated drinking water has caused increasingly frequent epidemics of hepatitis A, while between 8 percent and 10 percent of Romanians are believed to carry the virus for hepatitis B, which, like AIDS, is spread by contaminated blood transfusions, syringes, and unprotected sex. As of mid-1993, the government had registered 2,661 cases of AIDS, 2,481 of them children younger than 14. The health ministry denied Western news reports that some 3 million Romanians are infected with HIV, the virus believed to cause AIDS.

Romania has more than 49,000 doctors (including 6,500 dentists), making for a ratio of 2.2 doctors for every 1,000 people—not an impressive statistic. Medical professionals are also seriously underpaid, prompting many to emigrate abroad. Other problems in the health care system include the poor physical state of the nation's hospitals and clinics, and an antiquated pharmaceutical industry.

Romania's government appears to have insufficient resources to confront the crisis. Health care costs took up 3.9 percent of the country's gross domestic product in 1990. The share allocated to health expenditures in the cabinet's 1993 austerity budget was 8.2 percent. Privatization plays a major role in the government's plans for health care reform, but so far the country's pharmacies are the only sector to have been extensively privatized.

Some critics have charged that the health care system will be difficult to reform as long as the same people remain in charge of the process. As an example of the need for a change of personnel, the critics point out that Health Minister Iulian Mican reputedly was Ceausescu's personal physician and the main architect of the dictator's notorious "program of scientific nourishment," as the country's near-starvation diet of the 1980s was officially called.

NOTES

1. Michael Shafir, *RFE/RL*, April 30, 1993.
2. Roger Thurow, *Wall Street Journal*, October 20, 1994.
3. Gale Stokes, *The Walls Came Tumbling Down*, p. 58.
4. Eva Hoffman, *Exit into History: A Journey Through the New Eastern Europe*, p. 329.
5. Judith Ingram, *New York Times*, July 25, 1994.
6. Jane Perlez, *New York Times*, October 18, 1994.
7. Dan Ionescu *RFE/RL*, October 8, 1993.

10

Arts & Culture

For a nation of relatively small size, Romania has an impressive artistic and cultural heritage. All Romanians, from the humblest peasant to the most elite intellectual, take great pride in that achievement. In the words of musician Georges Enesco: "If only our administration and politics were on the same level as the arts, we would be one of the happiest countries on earth."[1]

Romania is also a well-educated country, in the sciences as well as the arts. The oldest school in the country, located at the monastery in Cenadul Vechi, dates from the 11th century. Today there are 48 institutions of higher learning (with 186 colleges), including 13 full universities, four technological universities, and many private institutes. The prior Communist regimes—although they tried to indoctrinate students with Marxist dogma—did provide free, universal, and compulsory education, and virtually eradicated illiteracy. (Today only 2.6 percent of the population 12 and older cannot read or write.) In the 1990s the educational system was reorganized to eliminate mandatory ideological training.

Shortly after the 1989 revolution, one writer noted: "Whoever talked to the new breed of Romanian students came away amazed by the breadth of their vision despite years of school-room indoctrination, by their courage, and by their language, refreshingly free of cant and the remnants of Marxist-Leninist cliches."[2]

The Communist era did have a significant, damaging impact on Romania's artistic and intellectual community. Only a few of its members were brave enough to become open dissidents during the Ceausescu dictatorship. Some went quietly into exile while most stayed behind to become either open or tacit collaborators with the regime. After the revolution, the dissident poet Mircea Dinescu was asked by a foreign journalist why the Romanian Writers' Union did not hold a tribunal to pass judgment on those members who had served as apologists for the Ceausescus. "But Madame," he replied, "that is half the entire Union and there are some very good writers among them."[3]

Although the dictator's wife Elena was widely viewed as a cruel, spiteful, and ignorant woman, Romania's leading intellectuals had to publicly pretend to believe the mythology that she was a world-class thinker and scientist. In some respects she became even more hated than her husband because of the baleful and repressive influence she wielded over the country's intellectual climate:

> Elena Ceausescu added a special poison, and it may be said that her bequest to the country was a traumatized intelligentsia. Asked after the revolution to explain her, a young writer could only mutter that it was impossible to understand how such a woman had existed in the twentieth century.[4]

In a similar vein, the former diplomat Mircea Codreanu asserted that had Elena lived, she should have been tried "for genocide not of people but of culture and education."[5]

Art, Music & Literature

Up until the 19th century, the creation of art in Romania was exclusively a religious occupation. This process reached its high point with the famous

15th- and 16th-century painted Orthodox churches and monasteries of Bukovina, in northern Moldavia, the exterior surfaces of which are decorated with beautiful frescoes illustrating Bible stories for the peasant faithful. In the modern period, however, Romania's most famous painters (who include Nicolae Grigorescu, Theodor Aman, Alexandru Ciucurencu, and Ion Tuculescu) have taken that heritage of folk and monastic art and combined it with more modern European motifs.

Romania's most famous artist is Constantin Brancusi (1876–1957), one of the world's greatest sculptors. He was born in a village near Tirgu Jiu in the region of Oltenia. At the age of seven he worked as a shepherd in the Carpathians, and later went on to higher education in Bucharest. He immigrated to Paris in 1904, where he gained international fame as a fixture of the modern art movement, pioneering abstract techniques of reducing sculpture to its "pure form" or essence. Despite his modernism, Brancusi gained much of his initial inspiration from the Romanian folk art and myths he was exposed to in his youth. Today most of his masterpieces are on display in France and the United States, although there is a popular "sculpture garden" of his works in Tirgu Jiu.

Georges Enesco (1881–1955)—composer, violinist, pianist, conductor, and teacher—is easily Romania's greatest contribution to the world of music. He incorporated Gypsy melodies in his Romanian Rhapsodies, as well as composing three symphonies and an opera.

Romania's literature before World War I consisted primarily of ballads, folk tales, and poems. "The Romanian is born a poet," is a sentiment often expressed in Romania.[6] Although underappreciated in his lifetime, Mikhai Eminescu is today considered the country's greatest 19th-century poet. Between World Wars I and II, a number of other poets achieved prominence, including George Bacovia, Tudor Arghezi, Ion Barbu, and Adrian Maniu. Two novelists who also became widely known were Eugen Lovinescu and Titu Maiorescu.

The most famous figure of the postwar period was playwright Eugène Ionesco, who in the late 1950s became one of the leading figures of the so-called theater of the absurd, which mixed elements of tragedy, comedy, and surrealism. Although he lived mostly in Paris and wrote in French, his world view was strongly shaped by the 13-year period he spent in Romania as a young man during its Fascist period. "The Ceausescus were just the latest in a line of farcical figures who have held power in Romania,"

A statue by Constantin Brancusi (1876–1957), considered one of the greatest sculptors of the modern era. Today most of his works are on display in France and the United States. (Romanian Cultural Center)

one Romanian has noted. "It's no accident . . . that Ionesco emerged from here. To him, theater of the absurd was merely theater of the real."

The Communist takeover brought a massive disruption in Romania's literary evolution as writers sought to cope with government censorship and restrictive Marxist views of art, problems that persisted for the next 40 years. Dumitru Radu Popescu became the most prominent writer of the 1960s, his novel *The Blue Lion* openly questioning the Communist regime. Among the few who openly stood up to Ceausescu in the 1970s and 1980s were poets Dinescu and Anna Blandiana and writer Paul Goma. Poet Nina Cassian and writer Norman Manea made names for themselves after going into exile in the United States.

Folk Culture

The folk art and folklore of Romania's peasant culture is among the richest and best preserved of Europe. Each region of the country has its own distinctive dress and crafts—including pottery, ceramics, rug-making, weaving, and woodcarving—as well as dancing and music. But even these ancient and enduring popular traditions were somewhat tainted by their use as standard props in government-sponsored propaganda exercises during the Ceausescu era, as Andrei Codrescu found when he returned from exile:

> I looked back and saw, coming around a bend on the road, a wide peasant cart drawn by two sturdy horses. The cart was loaded full of hay, and two peasants in long sheepskin coats sat over it, holding their whips like batons over the clippity-clop of hooves on hard snow. They were almost unbearably picturesque, like fake peasants in a pseudofolk tableau. They lifted their caps as they passed. Ceausescu's propaganda had made so much of the "peasant" that his reality was hard to fathom. One of the subtler crimes of nationalist propaganda is to make even the genuine unreal, to turn the world into postcard and caricature. One of the artistic tasks of the future will be to extract the peasant from the pseudopeasant, folk music from "folkloric ensembles," folk art from "popular socialist art."[7]

No discussion of popular culture would be complete without a brief introduction to Romania's delicious and exotic national cuisine. There is *ciorba*, a sour soup made from fermented bran, bacon, potatoes, and beef or chicken. Hearty stews such as *tochitura moldoveneasca* are often accompanied by *mamaliga*, a maize polenta. *Sarmale* is a spicy dish of bitter cabbage leaves stuffed with meat, and *mititei* are small grilled sausages perfumed with aromatic herbs. Among fish dishes, carp on the spit is a local specialty in the Danube delta region. Pork is the meat most commonly served. Indeed, a recent travel writer found that at many Romanian restaurants, "the litany of specials can sound like a Monty Python routine ('Pork, pork, pork, pork, pork . . . and I think we might also have some pork left')."[8]

A classic example of modern Romanian folk art: the "merry cemetery" in Sapanta, where carved headboards and humorous epitaphs commemorate the dead. (Romanian Tourist Board)

Sports

Romania is a sports-mad country. Even in rural areas one can often see endless groups of amateur athletes in fashionable warm-up suits jogging along the roadside. Romania has produced its own share of international sports stars, such as tennis player Ilie Nastase. More recently, a Romanian basketball player—7-foot, 7-inch Gheorghe Muresan—was picked in the 1994 National Basketball Association draft to play professionally in the United States with the Washington Bullets. But when most people think of Romanian sports, they probably think of the dozens of Olympic gold medals its women's gymnastics teams have won over the years, beginning with the famous victory of Nadia Comaneci at the 1976 Olympic Games.

Romania's gold medal–winning women's gymnastic team is honored at the 1984 Los Angeles Olympics. (AP/Wide World Photos)

Gheorghe Hagi, star player of Romania's national soccer team, celebrates after scoring a goal in the early rounds of the 1994 World Cup tournament, in which Romania advanced to the quarterfinals. (AP/Wide World Photos)

Nadia defected to the West shortly before the 1989 revolution. She quickly received bad press in the United States when she initially took up with a fellow Romanian escapee who turned out to be a married man, although the affair was short-lived. But she remained a national hero to most Romanians, a status that was reaffirmed when she made a triumphant return visit to Bucharest in 1995.

However, as in many countries in the world, the biggest sport in Romania is soccer. That obsession has grown even stronger in the wake of Romania's unexpected success at the 1994 World Cup, held in the United States. There Romania's national team, led by its star player Gheorghe Hagi, advanced to the quarterfinals only to lose to Sweden in a heartbreaker; after battling to a 2-2 tie, Sweden won 5-4 in the sudden death penalty kick shootout. For all the problems and divisions in Romanian society, the glorious near-triumph was a moment that brought the entire country together in joyous celebration.

NOTES

1. Norman Manea, *On Clowns: The Dictator and the Artist*, p. 17.
2. Edward Behr, *Kiss the Hand You Cannot Bite*, p. 278.
3. Mark Frankland, *The Patriots' Revolution*, p. 314.
4. Ibid, p. 312.
5. Behr, op. cit., p. 275.
6. Manea, op. cit., p. 17.
7. Andrei Codrescu, *The Hole in the Flag*, p. 151.
8. Jack Barth, *Travel & Leisure*, December 1994.

11

Foreign Policy

Romania's foreign policy has been one of the nation's few unequivocal successes of the post-communist era. After a slow start, the new government has used the country's traditional diplomatic skills to take full advantage of post–Cold War opportunities to improve its relations with most of its neighbors and reach a rapprochement with Western Europe and the United States. By portraying itself as a relatively stable anchor in a troubled region, Romania has managed to escape the isolation of the Ceausescu era and reassert itself as a useful player on the world stage.

The process did not begin smoothly, however. In the 1990–92 period, the leading Western nations essentially put Romania on "probation." They warned the new government in Bucharest that it would have to improve its domestic record on political and economic reforms and human rights if it wanted to join the international community as a member in good standing. Because of its slowness to make such necessary changes, Romania fell far behind the other formerly Communist countries of Eastern Europe in the amount of trade, aid, and investment it received from the West.

The new government really had only itself to blame, as Nestor Ratesh noted:

> In December 1989, Romania gained the world's affection as never before. It soon lost it. The power of the former Communists, the shadowy presence of the security police, the political and ethnic violence, the rough treatment of the opposition, and the government control of the radio and television all combined to undermine the postrevolutionary leadership's credibility abroad, especially in the West. In a few months, the precious capital of goodwill was mindlessly dissipated.[1]

Many Romanians tended, as usual, to place the blame on outsiders rather than themselves. A leading Bucharest journalist exclaimed: "A new martyrdom begins for Romania. No sooner has the burden [of Ceausescu] been lifted, albeit incompletely, than another heavier cross is put upon its shoulders . . . the Cross of humiliation." Was the country that had "uprooted totalitarianism . . . in just one wink of history" now to become "a victim on the altar of its own victory"? Romanians would not go begging at the "high imperial courts" of the West, he declared.[2]

European Integration, U.S. Approval

Initially, the United States took an even harder line against the "new" Romania than did its European allies. In the aftermath of Ceausescu's overthrow in December 1989, Washington appeared to find fault with the "neocommunist" character of the new regime. Secretary of State James Baker III was the last senior Western official to visit Bucharest in the wake of the revolution, and he stayed for only a few hours. The United States extended $80 million in humanitarian assistance, but over the next few years resisted rewarding Romania with long-term economic aid and the coveted most favored nation (MFN) trading status. In addition, U.S. leaders tended to distance themselves from senior Romanian officials at diplomatic gatherings.

By contrast, Western Europe took a more pragmatic, "business-as-usual" approach, feeling that the best way to change Romania's behavior was with hands-on engagement. French President François Mitterrand became the first Western head of state to visit Bucharest in April 1991, and a year later Romania and Germany signed a treaty of friendship and cooperation. The leading European powers were motivated in part by the perception that Romania, for all its internal imperfections, remained a bulwark between the growing chaos to the west—where Yugoslavia was descending into bloody civil war—and the east, where the Soviet Union had dissolved into a patchwork of quarrelsome mini-states.

These fears were skillfully played upon by Romanian diplomats, led by Adrian Nastase, who served as foreign minister from 1990 to 1992, and his successor Teodor Melescanu. Their first major coup came in February 1993 when, after many months of negotiations, Romania became the fourth former Communist country to sign an association agreement with the European Community (EC). Premier Nicolae Vacaroiu signed the accord in his first trip abroad as Romania's head of government.

The EC began as an organization for economic cooperation between Western European nations. But more recently it has evolved into a force for political integration as well, a process that reached a milestone in November 1993 when the Maastricht Treaty took effect and the EC became the European Union (EU). The practical effect of Romania's association agreement would be to eliminate trade barriers between it and the EU over a 10-year period. But the accord also had an important symbolic value, as it began the process of ushering Romania into the political structures of modern Europe.

Another key step in that process came in October 1993, when Romania finally won admission to the Council of Europe as its 32nd full member. The Council of Europe, based in Strasbourg, France, is primarily a symbolic body, but membership in it is widely seen as a "passport" to other European political and economic institutions. Doubts about Romania's human rights record, particularly its treatment of its Hungarian (Magyar) minority, were the main reason that Romania was the last former

Eastern bloc country to gain admission to the council. During months of hard negotiations Romania was compelled to promise to improve its record, and its membership won final approval in a meeting of the council's Committee of Ministers in which the Hungarian ambassador abstained in the voting.

Afterward, President Ion Iliescu addressed the Council of Europe at a summit in Vienna, Austria. He said Romania's admission would "give new impetus to the country's political life," but warned against "replacing the old ideological Iron Curtain by new economic barriers between the poor East and the rich West." He added that Romania was determined to "reject categorically any manifestation of racism, xenophobia, anti-Semitism, and intolerance, including all forms of religious discrimination."[3]

There were some critical voices. A member of Romania's political opposition asserted that the government could no longer behave like "a pupil whose main concern is to cheat his teacher . . . We still look upon the Council of Europe as an adversary or a political rival, not as a family into which we are accepted with all rights and obligations."[4] And an opposition newspaper in Bucharest called the country's admission "'an almost unexpected gulp of oxygen' for Romanian citizens, who henceforth have the right to appeal to the council if they believe their rights are violated at home."[5] That right was quickly demonstrated in early 1994 when the council announced an inquiry into civil liberties in Romania.

In January 1994 Romania became the first former member of the Warsaw Pact—the Soviet-led defense alliance that dissolved in 1991—to sign an agreement with the North Atlantic Treaty Organization (NATO) under its new Partnership for Peace (PFP) program. NATO was the U.S.-led alliance that had faced off against the Soviet bloc during the long years of the Cold War. NATO had designed the partnership as a means of reassuring the new Eastern European governments without granting them full membership in NATO, a move Moscow warned it would view as a threat to its security. Partnership members would not be entitled to automatic protection under NATO's defensive umbrella, but would be able to join NATO in joint military exercises, peacekeeping missions, training, and defense planning. Romania's political opposition, while welcoming the new arrangement, warned that the growing coalition between the ruling regime and extremist parties might jeopardize the country's integration into NATO structures.

Romania's growing acceptance in Europe helped improve its relations with the United States as well. Earlier, Romania had garnered considerable goodwill from Washington during the Persian Gulf conflict of 1990–91. Romania had fortuitously taken over the rotating presidency of the United Nations Security Council a day before the Iraqi invasion of Kuwait and skillfully used its position to support the U.S.-led alliance against Iraq. The diplomatic respect it gained as a result was widely seen as having offset the large economic losses Romania suffered as a result of the U.N.'s trade sanctions against Iraq.

The gradual thaw in U.S.-Romanian relations grew warmer still in October 1993, when the U.S. Congress voted in favor of ratifying a bilateral trade agreement that would include restoration of most favored nation trading status, long a key goal of Romanian foreign policy. That was followed in 1994 by a visit to Washington by President Iliescu, where he met with President Bill Clinton.

A Good Neighbor Policy?

Romania understandably views itself as living in a rough neighborhood. Thus its efforts to improve its relations with Western Europe and the United States (aside from achieving economic benefits) are aimed at gaining protection against its historic enemies, such as Russia, Hungary, and Bulgaria.

Romania was the first former Soviet bloc nation to sign a treaty of friendship with Russia, which committed both countries to respect their mutual territorial integrity and the inviolability of their current borders. But bilateral tensions persisted over the issue of the former Soviet republic of Moldova, which gained its independence in 1991. Moldova controls most of the territory of the former Romanian province of Bessarabia (Ukraine controls the rest), which was part of Greater Romania between the world wars. The majority of its population consists of ethnic Romanians, although there is a significant minority of ethnic Slavs, both Russians and Ukrainians.

There is a strong popular feeling among nationalist Romanians that Moldova should once again be reunited with its motherland. Anti-Russian slogans such as "Jackboots out of Moldova!" and "Russia is yours, Romania is ours" were commonly heard in Bucharest after the 1989 revolution.[6] The Romanian government established diplomatic relations with Moldova in 1991 and steered clear of openly calling for reunification to avoid antagonizing Moscow. But in 1992 a civil war erupted when separatist Russians and Ukrainians in the eastern, primarily Slavic region of Trans-Dniester broke away from Moldova and declared independence. The Russian military lent support to the rebels, while Romania was reported to have supplied arms to the Moldovan forces.

The fighting ended in a stalemate, although Trans-Dniester retained de facto autonomy. In recent years, Moscow has made moves to improve its relations with Moldova and withdraw support for the separatists. Meanwhile, Moldova held a national referendum in March 1994 in which some 95 percent of participating voters backed an independent state rather than union with Romania. That appeared to quash any remaining hopes in Bucharest for a merger between the two countries, at least for the foreseeable future.

Other territorial claims complicated Romania's relations with Ukraine and Bulgaria. Ukraine reacted angrily when Romanian nationalists raised the issue of former Romanian territories that Ukraine gained control of as a result of World War II, and Bulgaria accused Bucharest of having territorial designs on the region of southern Dobruja.

Despite these difficulties, Romania forged ahead with an energetic program of diplomacy in 1992, opening an embassy in the Ukrainian capital of Kiev, concluding a treaty with Bulgaria, and signing a series of agreements with Turkey and Greece. And in the most significant development, in June 1992 Romania and 10 of its neighbors (including six former Soviet republics) signed the so-called Declaration of Istanbul, which provided for the creation of a new zone of peaceful economic activity. This Black Sea Economic Cooperation Group was aimed at encouraging trade and developing transport and infrastructure in the region.

Romania was motivated to improve its relations with its neighbors in part to compensate for the growing instability in the Balkans, the main reason for which was the civil wars that ripped apart Yugoslavia beginning in the early 1990s. Bucharest tried to present itself as a mediator in the conflicts between the rump Yugoslav federation (consisting of Serbia and

Montenegro) and the newly independent republics of Croatia and Bosnia-Herzegovina.

The situation was complicated by Romania's efforts to enforce the U.N. embargo on Yugoslavia by preventing Serbia-bound vessels from proceeding up the Danube River. In late 1992 and early 1993, Serbian authorities retaliated by blockading the Danube, detaining Romanian tugboats and barges, and ordering the giant lock at the Iron Gates hydroelectric station to be closed to Romanian vessels. This so-called "ship-and-locks war"[7] caused major economic losses to Romania and seemed to have a sobering effect on Bucharest. Although Romania reaffirmed its commitment to upholding the U.N. sanctions, it proceeded in April 1994 to sign a treaty with Yugoslavia—which had become an international pariah state—on bilateral political relations.

The final major stumbling block to regional cooperation was the long-festering dispute between Romania and Hungary over Transylvania. Romania believed that Hungary still hoped to regain the territory and was using Transylvania's Magyar minority as a subversive "fifth column" to further that ultimate goal. Hungary in turn complained continually about what it saw as the Romanian government's political and cultural oppression of its ethnic brethren in Transylvania.

Nevertheless, both countries seemed determined to reach some sort of compromise in order to avoid hindering their efforts to gain greater integration into Europe. In September 1993 Geza Jeszenszky became the first Hungarian foreign minister to pay an official visit to Bucharest since 1989, and Romania's Foreign Minister Teodor Melescanu followed with a visit to Budapest in September 1994. No diplomatic breakthroughs were achieved in the long-awaited effort to complete a bilateral treaty. But it was agreed that any accord should include guarantees that Budapest would relinquish any territorial claims to Transylvania, and Romania would respect the rights of its Hungarian minority.

Both countries had their work cut out for them, and Romania in particular faced a hard road in convincing its citizens that Hungary could ever be a friendly neighbor. A 1993 public opinion poll indicated that 59 percent of Romanians believed Hungary was "dangerous" to their country. Another survey found that 41 percent of those polled considered Hungary a potential aggressor, while 17 percent feared Russia, 9 percent Yugoslavia, and 3 percent Ukraine.[8]

NOTES

1. Nestor Ratesh, *Romania: The Entangled Revolution*, pp. 148–149.
2. Mark Frankland, *The Patriots' Revolution*, p. 194.
3. Dan Ionescu, *RFE/RL*, November 5, 1993.
4. Ibid.
5. Ibid.
6. Ratesh, op. cit., p. 151.
7. Dan Ionescu, *RFE/RL*, March 9, 1993.
8. Dan Ionescu, *RFE/RL*, October 22, 1993.

12

Future Prospects

Whither Romania? A simple question, impossible to answer simply. There are many factors to consider: historical, political, economic, and social. The key will be the Romanian people themselves. They have a tendency, which is natural enough considering their tortured history, to look to outside forces either to save them or to blame for their misfortune. But they will have to look to their own inner strengths as a people if they are to escape from their long cycle of troubles.

A young Romanian economist has put the matter eloquently:

> Nobody knows how to do the transition in Romania because there's no social base, no traditions from which to start. The problem is a lack of a lived collective experience. In Poland, there was a decade of Solidarity [the labor union that led the struggle against communism].

> People learned how to get together, how to act on their own. That's
> why their reform got off the ground so quickly. Here, we don't know
> how to trust each other. We have this habit of waiting for the
> authorities to solve everything. Or we keep waiting for the West to
> come to the rescue. Well, we've waited, and the West isn't coming.
> We have to learn how to do things ourselves.[1]

It has been said that the story of Romania is a concrete illustration of
the Sisyphus myth, the ancient Greek tale of the king who was punished
by having to continually roll a huge boulder up a hill, only to have it roll
back down to the bottom each time he reached the summit. Romania's
history is replete with such reversals, especially in this century. The dream
of Greater Romania is born after World War I but disappears after World
War II amid a Soviet-imposed Communist takeover. Hopes are briefly
reawakened by a breakaway from the Soviet model but quickly dashed
by the descent into the darkness of the Ceausescu dictatorship. Finally,
with the 1989 revolution Romanian society is once again put in the position
of starting all over from scratch.

Romania has largely dropped off the world's radar screen in recent
years. As was suggested earlier, the paucity of international news coverage
is in some ways a good thing. It indicates that life in Romania has achieved
a kind of dull normalcy, mostly free of the disasters and violent strife that
create sensational headlines. But there is also the danger that the country
will slip back into mysterious obscurity, so that all the world will remember
is its history of figurative vampires, from Vlad the Impaler to Nicolae
Ceausescu.

Like many Romanians, President Ion Iliescu has expressed unhappiness
with what he perceives to be distorted pictures of his country's history
and current situation. At a 1994 scientific conference in Sinaia he addressed
the issue:

> There is an anti-Romanian lobby showing a false image of reality. Of
> course we have difficulties, of course we are going through a rough
> period, of course people have many reasons to be dissatisfied. We
> have the burdensome heritage of the past to deal with, plus the
> specific difficulties of the transition, but, as you can see, we do not
> live in a wilderness. People do not get killed in the street, as some
> say abroad, and this nation is not only made up of handicapped
> citizens. The Romanian people are wise, we have a long history

Romania's future: A six-year-old picks up and relights a fallen candle at the Revolution Square memorial in Bucharest. (AP/Wide World Photos)

behind us, during which we have accumulated many spiritual and material assets. The Romanians have always had an intellectual potential that made it possible for us to overcome many historical tribulations, over and over again. This is our greatest quality, our inner strength and our creative potential. It has always represented a valuable asset in this world and we must enhance it now.[2]

More than its intellectual and scientific assets, however, what Romania now needs to develop most of all are its political, economic, and social structures and attitudes. The groundwork is there—a flourishing if fractious political opposition, a mostly free press, a growing independent labor movement—but it must be nurtured further to bring the country fully into the modern community of nations.

Most observers agree that a key step would be for the minority leftist government to forgo its growing reliance on extremist parties that echo the worst strains of Romanian history—communism and fascism—and instead learn to work with the mainstream political opposition. That would call for a rooting out of the influence of Ceausescu holdovers and an end to the practice of covert "Securitate politics." It would also require that all respectable public figures take a concrete stand against racism in any form, whether directed against Jews, Gypsies, Hungarians, or any other group.

There are no easy economic answers. Romania has chosen to move toward a free-market capitalist system with calculated slowness, avoiding the harsh "shock therapy" approach taken by Poland and Russia. But the small-scale entrepreneurship that is beginning to catch on in the agricultural and service sectors will have to be followed up with the much-delayed privatization of the industrial economy if the country is to attract the foreign investment it so desperately needs. Romania's well-educated and industrious work force will doubtless prove to be a major national asset when and if the economy finally begins to take off.

And so the main question emerges: Will the 1989 revolution be carried through and completed, so that Romania can join modern Europe in both the political and economic realms, or will the country allow itself to backslide into the conflict and stagnation that have so often typified its history? The glorious month of December 1989 "was a revolution in people's souls when they suddenly felt no more fear," Andrei Codrescu has written. "This revolution is going on still. Whoever let the tiger out of its cage is in no position to put it back again."[3] From that perspective, it seems clear that any prognosis of Romania's future has to remain cautiously optimistic.

NOTES

1. Eva Hoffman, *Exit into History: A Journey Through the New Eastern Europe*, pp. 293–294.
2. *Romanian Panorama*, 8–9 (36–37), 1994, p. 12.
3. Andrei Codrescu, *The Hole in the Flag*, p. 238.

Chronology of Romanian History

The Pre-Modern Era

A.D. 101–106:	Kingdom of Dacia conquered by Roman emperor Trajan
A.D. 271:	Emperor Aurelian orders Roman withdrawal
3rd–6th centuries:	Succession of invasions by barbarian tribes from the East
896:	Magyars arrive in Hungary and subsequently absorb Transylvania
1360:	Moldavia declares independence from Hungary
1380:	Walachia follows suit
1386–1418:	Rule of Mircea the Old in Walachia
1437:	Transylvania's noblemen form Union of Three Nations
1456–62:	Rule of Vlad Tepes (the Impaler) in Walachia

1457–1504:	Rule of Stephen the Great in Moldavia
1521–41:	Ottoman Turks consolidate control of Romanian lands
1593–1601:	Rule of Michael the Brave, who briefly unites Romania
1699:	Uniate Church founded in Transylvania
1711–16:	Turks institute Phanariot system in Moldavia and Walachia
1711–1856:	Russia, Austria, and Ottoman Empire wage wars on Romanian soil
1821:	Revolt ends Phanariot system

The Modern Era

1859–66:	Rule of Alexander Cuza
1861:	Union of Moldavia and Walachia
1866–1914:	Rule of King Carol I
1881:	Kingdom of Romania declared
1907:	Peasant revolt crushed
1912–13:	1st and 2nd Balkan Wars fought
1914–27:	Rule of King Ferdinand I
1918:	World War I ends. Greater Romania formed
1921:	Romanian Communist Party (RCP) founded
1930–40:	Rule of King Carol II
June–August 1940:	Greater Romania dismembered at start of World War II
September 1940:	Fascist Marshal Ion Antonescu seizes power
August 1944:	King Michael ousts Antonescu in anti-German coup; Soviet army moves in

The Communist Era

March 6, 1945:	Pro-Communist Petru Groza named premier
October 1945:	Gheorghe Gheorghiu-Dej becomes Romanian Communist Party general secretary
November 1946:	RCP wins power in fraudulent elections
February 10, 1947:	Treaty of Paris recognizes Romania's postwar borders
December 30, 1947:	King Michael forced to abdicate; People's Republic of Romania proclaimed
March 1948:	RCP consolidates power in national elections
1948–62:	Agricultural system forcibly collectivized
1952:	Gheorghiu-Dej consolidates position as undisputed leader
1956:	Romania begins to chart international course independent of Soviet Union
April 26, 1964:	Central Committee issues "Declaration of Independence" from Moscow
March 19, 1965:	Gheorghiu-Dej dies; succeeded by triumvirate from which Nicolae Ceausescu ultimately emerges on top
1967:	Romania establishes relations with West Germany; retains ties with Israel after Six Day War
1968:	Ceausescu wins Western praise by opposing Soviet invasion of Czechoslovakia
1971:	Ceausescus visit China and North Korea; are inspired to create cult of personality and "pharaonic socialism"
1988:	Rural "systemization" program prompts crisis with Hungary; Ceausescu renounces most favored nation (MFN) trading status with U.S.
March 1989:	"Letter of Six" criticizing Ceausescu issued by former leading officials
December 15–20, 1989:	Timisoara racked by protests and bloodshed
December 22–25, 1989:	Unrest spreads to Bucharest; Ceausescus flee and are captured; National Salvation Front (NSF) proclaimed
December 25, 1989:	Nicolae and Elena Ceausescu executed

The Post-Communist Era

1990

January:	Anticommunist protests against NSF erupt
May 20:	NSF triumphs in mostly free elections; Ion Iliescu becomes president
June 14–15:	Government imports Jiu Valley coal miners to crush opposition and "restore order"
August:	National Agency for Privatization set up
November:	Price increases prompt 100,000-strong protest in Bucharest

1991

September:	Jiu Valley miners return to confront government; Premier Petre Roman forced to resign and is replaced by Theodor Stolojan
November:	Parliament approves new constitution defining Romania as a multiparty presidential republic with a free-market economy
December:	New constitution endorsed by 77 percent of voters in national referendum

1992

February–March:	Local elections confirm decline in popularity of NSF
March:	NSF formally splits into two parties; leftist faction retains power while centrist faction goes into opposition
April:	Exiled King Michael receives tumultuous welcome during brief visit to Bucharest
June:	Romania joins 11-nation Black Sea Economic Cooperation Group

September:	Ruling Democratic National Salvation Front (DNSF) hangs onto power in national elections
October:	Iliescu wins presidential runoff vote
November:	Nicolae Vacaroiu named premier

1993

February:	Romania signs association agreement with the European Community
July:	DNSF merges with smaller leftist parties to form ruling Party of Social Democracy in Romania (PSDR)
October:	Romania wins admission to the Council of Europe
November:	Huge pro-economic reform protest staged in Bucharest

1994

January:	Romania joins NATO's Partnership for Peace program
April:	The national currency, the leu, is "floated" (becomes internally convertible with other currencies)
August:	Extremist right-wing Party of Romanian National Unity (PRNU) officially joins government
October:	King Michael denied entry at Bucharest airport

1995

| January: | Ruling PSDR formally cements alliance with three extremist ultranationalist parties |

Bibliography

Books

Bachman, Ronald D., ed. *Romania: A Country Study*. Washington, D.C.: Library of Congress, 1991.

Banac, Ivo, ed. *Eastern Europe in Revolution*. Ithaca, N.Y.: Cornell University Press, 1992.

Basdevant, Denise. *Against Tide and Tempest: The Story of Romania*. New York: Robert Spellers & Sons, 1965.

Behr, Edward. *Kiss the Hand You Cannot Bite: The Rise and Fall of the Ceausescus*. New York: Villard Books, 1991.

Bobango, Gerald J. *The Emergence of the Romanian National State*. Boulder, Colo.: East European Quarterly, 1979.

Brown, Aurel. *Romanian Foreign Policy Since 1965*. New York: Praeger, 1978.

Brown, J. F. *Eastern Europe and Communist Rule*. Durham, N.C.: Duke University Press, 1988.

155

————. *The New Eastern Europe: The Khrushchev Era and After*. New York: Praeger, 1966.

Cipkowski, Peter. *Revolution in Eastern Europe*. New York: John Wiley & Sons, 1991.

Codrescu, Andrei. *The Hole in the Flag: A Romanian Exile's Story of Return and Revolution*. New York: William Morrow, 1991.

Fischer-Galati, Stephen. *The New Rumania: From People's Democracy to Socialist Republic*. Cambridge, Mass.: MIT Press, 1967.

Frankland, Mark. *The Patriots' Revolution: How Eastern Europe Toppled Communism and Won Its Freedom*. Chicago: Ivan Dee, 1992.

Giurescu, Constantin C. *Transylvania in the History of Romania: An Historical Outline*. London: Garnstone Press.

Gursan-Salzman. *The Last Jews of Radauti*. Garden City, N.Y.: Doubleday, 1983.

Hale, Julian. *The Land and People of Romania*. Philadelphia: J.B. Lippincott, 1972.

Hoffman, Charles. *Gray Dawn: The Jews of Eastern Europe in the Post-Communist Era*. New York: HarperCollins, 1992.

Hoffman, Eva. *Exit into History: A Journey Through the New Eastern Europe*. New York: Viking, 1993.

Jagendorf, Siegfried. *Jagendorf's Foundry: A Memoir of the Romanian Holocaust, 1941–1944*. New York: HarperCollins, 1991.

Laufer, Peter. *Iron Curtain Rising*. San Francisco: Mercury House, 1991.

Lendvai, Paul. *Eagles in Cobwebs: Nationalism and Communism in the Balkans*. Garden City, N.Y.: Doubleday, 1969.

Manea, Norman. *On Clowns: The Dictator and the Artist*. New York: Grove Weidenfeld, 1992.

Otetea, Andrei, ed. *The History of the Romanian People*. New York: Twayne Publishers, 1970.

Ratesh, Nestor. *Romania: The Entangled Revolution*. New York: Praeger & the Center for Strategic and International Studies, 1991.

Shafir, Michael. *Romania—Politics, Economics and Society: Political Stagnation and Simulated Change*. Boulder, Colo.: Lynne Rienner Publishers, 1985.

Stokes, Gale. *The Walls Came Tumbling Down: The Collapse of Communism in Eastern Europe*. New York: Oxford University Press, 1993.

Tismaneanu, Vladimir. *Reinventing Politics: Eastern Europe from Stalin to Havel*. New York: Macmillan, 1992.

Periodicals

(Note: In the listings below, *Radio Free Europe/Radio Liberty Research Reports* has been abbreviated as *RFE/RL*. Beginning in 1995 that journal became *Transition*.)

Barany, Zoltan. "Grim Realities in Eastern Europe." *Transition*, March 29, 1995, 3–8.

Barth, Jack. "In Search of Dracula." *Travel & Leisure*, December 1994, 82.

Binder, David. "European Gypsies Issue Call For Human Rights." *New York Times*, May 2, 1993, A12.

Codrescu, Andrei. "Fascism on a Pedestal." *New York Times*, December 7, 1993, A27.

Economist, Editors of. "Isarescued." *Economist*, July 9, 1994, 53.

Henry, David C. "Reviving Romania's Rural Economy." *RFE/RL*, February 18, 1994, 18–24.

Ingram, Judith. "Now Romania Aids Orphans At Its Hearth." *New York Times*, July 25, 1994, A9.

Ionescu, Dan. "Birth Pangs of Privatization." *Transition*, April 14, 1995, 47–51.

————. "UM 0215: A Controversial Intelligence Service in Romania." *RFE/RL*, July 29, 1994, 27–30.

————. "Personnel Changes in the Romanian Intelligence Service." *RFE/RL*, July 8, 1994, 22–25.

————. "Romania Adjusting to NATO's Partnership for Peace Program." *RFE/RL*, March 4, 1994, 43–47.

————. "Romania's Privatization Program: Who Is in Charge?" *RFE/RL*, February 4, 1994, 28–34.

————. "Romania's Currency Plummeting." *RFE/RL*, December 10, 1993, 43–48.

————. "Romania Admitted to the Council of Europe." *RFE/RL*, November 5, 1993, 40–45.

————. "Still No Breakthrough in Romanian-Hungarian Relations." *RFE/RL*, October 22, 1993, 26–32.

————. "Health Care Crisis: Romania." *RFE/RL*, October 8, 1993, 60–62.

————. "The Balkan Conflict: Romania's Quandary." *RFE/RL*, March 9, 1993, 13–17.

————. "Romania Signs Association Agreement with the EC." *RFE/RL*, March 5, 1993, 33–37.

————. "Romania's Winter of Shortages." *RFE/RL*, February 5, 1993, 45–48.

Kamm, Henry. "End of Communism Worsens Anti-Gypsy Racism." *New York Times*, November 17, 1993, A12.

————. "Death Is a Neighbor, and the Gypsies Are Terrified." *New York Times*, October 27, 1993, A4.

Nash, Nathaniel C. "From Communist Vineyards, a Bouquet of Iodine." *New York Times*, March 8, 1995, A4.

————. "Coke's Great Romanian Adventure." *New York Times*, February 26, 1995, F1.

Ottaway, David B. "Post-Communist Country a Pre-Industrial Time Warp." *Washington Post*, August 1, 1994, A17.

————. "A Battle for Identity Divides Transylvania." *Washington Post*, July 5, 1994, A12.

Perlez, Jane. "Uprising or Coup? Romanians Ask 5 Years Later." *New York Times*, December 25, 1994, A3.

————. "Where Communists Trampled, a Village Rises." *New York Times*, October 18, 1994, A4.

————. "Romanian Leader Calls Ex-King a Threat." *New York Times*, October 13, 1994, A5.

————. "A Suitably Opaque Talk With Romania's Top Spy." *New York Times*, November 30, 1993, A4.

————. "Bleak Romanian Economy Growing Ever Bleaker." *New York Times*, November 24, 1993, A3.

Shafir, Michael. "Ruling Party Formalizes Relations With Extremists." *Transition*, April 14, 1995, 42–46.

————. "Immigrants in Romania." *RFE/RL*, June 24, 1994, 41–46.

————. "Romania." *RFE/RL*, April 22, 1994, 87–94.

————. "Best-selling Spy Novels Seek to Rehabilitate Romanians' Securitate." *RFE/RL*, November 12, 1993, 14–18.

————. "The Caritas Affair: A Transylvanian 'Eldorado.'" *RFE/RL*, September 24, 1993, 23–27.

————. "Romanians and the Transition to Democracy." *RFE/RL*, April 30, 1993, 42–48.

————. "Growing Political Extremism in Romania." *RFE/RL*, April 2, 1993, 18–25.

Shafir, Michael, and Dan Ionescu. "Romania: A Crucially Uneventful Year." *RFE/RL*, January 7, 1994, 122–126.

———. "Romania: Political Change and Economic Malaise." *RFE/RL*, January 1, 1993, 108–112.

Thurow, Roger. "Miners Can Move Mountains in Romania." *Wall Street Journal*, October 20, 1994, A19.

Washington Post, Editors of. "Transcript of the Closed Trial of Nicolae and Elena Ceausescu." *Washington Post*, December 29, 1989, A26.

INDEX

Entries are filed letter by letter. *Italic* page references indicate illustrations and captions. Roman numerals and page references followed by *m* indicate maps. Locators followed by *c* indicate chronology.

DATE DUE			